THE DOOR TO MORE

Foreword by **SAMUEL RODRIGUEZ**

THE DOOR TO MORE

TONY STEWART

General Director of Publications: David W. Ray
Managing Editor of Publications: Lance Colkmire
Executive Assistant: Elaine McDavid
Cover Design: Justin Johnson
Layout Design: Michael McDonald

ISBN: 978-1-64288-194-3

Visit *www.pathwaypress.org* for more information.

ENDORSEMENTS

The Door to More reminds us all that we will encounter open doors, closed doors, and locked doors. God knows what's on the other side of each, and He will guide you if you stay close to Him.

—Jentezen Franklin
Senior Pastor, Free Chapel
New York Times *best-selling author*

In his new book, *The Door to More*, my friend Tony Stewart explains the various kinds of doors we encounter in our lifetime. Some people choose to avoid doors altogether, thinking that staying where they are involves no risk. However, God never intended for you to stay where you are or the way you are right now. He desires for you to experience more of His presence, His power, and His blessing. Tony brilliantly outlines the revelation you need to step through the door to more with boldness and confidence.

—Dr. Rod Parsley
Pastor and Founder, World Harvest Church
Columbus, Ohio

The life of a Christian believer is a series of doors and the opportunities they represent. It is our spiritual challenge to discern these symbolic doors, whether they be open pathways or an idea slammed shut. In *The Door to More*, Pastor Tony Stewart provides Biblically based guidance and instruction in crossing these thresholds into greater glory.

—Dr. Tim Hill
Church of God General Overseer
Cleveland, Tennessee

My brother Tony has written such a prescient and necessary read for everyone who's ever wondered what their role and gift might be. We can all open doors for others. Tony didn't just come up with a cool concept; he has lived, bled, sweated, and cried this message. The tireless and selfless way he has opened doors for me and so many like me over-qualifies him to speak directly to your life and future!

—Israel Houghton
Grammy award winning recording artist

I have known my good friend Tony Stewart for a long time. Hence, I know firsthand how he has seized open doors of opportunity and overcome the disappointment of closed doors. I have no doubt *The Door to More* will encourage, inspire, and motivate you to push past complacency and step into your next season.

—Dr. Sam Chand
Best-selling author and leadership expert

As a believer trying to follow God's will, I have lived my life going through open doors, trying to understand closed doors, and always anticipating new doors of opportunity. In Pastor Tony Stewart's new book, he helps answer the questions about spiritual doors in our lives. I believe in the season we are living, we must be fine-tuned to know clearly what doors are the correct to go through. This book will bring understanding and insight that you need to make right decisions that line up with the Word of God.

—Joni Lamb

Co-founder, Daystar Television Network

When designing a building, architects carefully construct a plan to ensure that doors are properly placed. These entrances and exits have great power—to open possibilities or shut for your protection. Likewise, in the spiritual realm, we encounter doors every day. In *The Door to More*, my good friend Tony Stewart inspires us to look at these doors from another perspective. As you read this book, your spiritual eyes will open, and you will begin recognizing the doors God has placed in front of you. I pray you will have the courage to walk through the door to more.

—Dr. Dave Martin

Pastor, Motor City Church
Detroit, Michigan

CONTENTS

FOREWORD . . . 11

INTRODUCTION . . . 13

1 THE POWER OF A DOORWAY . . . 17

2 HOW TO ATTRACT THE PRESENCE OF GOD . . . 31

3 CAN YOU SEE IT? . . . 51

4 THE POWER OF PARTNERSHIP . . . 65

5 IT'S TIME TO STRETCH . . . 83

6 USE WHAT'S IN YOUR HAND . . . 101

7 SEIZE THE MOMENT . . . 117

8 IT'S YOUR TIME . . . 133

FOREWORD

We enter through doors every day. From bedroom to kitchen. From the house into morning light and into the car for our daily commute. From the chilly night air into the familiar warmth of a family home after a long day. These are, of course, physical doors in our life that lead from one place to another. Yet there also are invisible spiritual doors all around us. Sometimes God opens them. Sometimes He locks them. Often He leaves it up to us whether to enter or exit.

How do we find these doors? And how do we decide if we should go through them? After all, not all of them lead to the same place, and just because there is a door does not mean we ought to go through it. Sometimes *when* we go through a door matters as much as *where* it leads. In *The Door to More*, my friend Tony Stewart opens Scripture to teach us how to see the doors around us with spiritual eyes.

The story of Noah reminds us it sometimes takes faith to see the other side of the doorway. David challenges us to seize the moment when the right time comes and the door swings open before us. Paul shows us we should not walk lightly through a door just because it is open—often, we will face challenges on the other side.

Once we start recognizing these doorways, it may be intimidating to think about them. As humans, we tend to overthink what is before us. But Tony reminds us that whatever may be awaiting us, we can cross every threshold with Spirit-filled confidence, knowing God is with us.

—Samuel Rodriguez
Lead pastor, New Season Church

President/CEO of *National Hispanic Christian Leadership Conference*

Author of *Persevere With Power: What Heaven Starts, Hell Cannot Stop!*

Executive producer of the movies *Breakthrough* and *Flamin' Hot*

INTRODUCTION

Do you feel change is on the horizon, in your not-too-distant future, or maybe even knocking at your door?

That's good news: You are standing at the doorway of a new season with greater possibilities than you've ever had before!

The reality is we all change, and change is necessary for growth and, in many cases, even survival. The challenges of change, the constancy of change, and the cost of change can be overwhelming, however. What we are settling into and embracing today is changing in our tomorrow, and the adjustment and challenges it demands of us at times seems more than we can handle and bear.

The cost—mentally, emotionally, and spiritually—of change seems more than we can afford. I find the most challenging times of change in my life, family, and ministry are in seasons of comfort and familiarity, when I don't want to change or even see or feel the need for change. The reality is, it's in those times that I probably need change the most. When things are comfortable and too familiar, my life is less fruitful and change is required.

God's plan is always progressive; it is always defining, aligning, preparing and even repairing us when needed for something greater that is in our future. His plan moves us from glory to glory, season to season, to embrace the prophetic declaration the Father has spoken over our lives. The challenge is navigating, embracing, and stepping into those moments with faith and expectation—moments that unlock and lead to new seasons of abundance and fruitfulness.

The good news is the Father has given us a manual for embracing changing culture and times, a roadmap on how to navigate from one season to the next; it is called the Bible. From Genesis to Revelation—from the beginning to the end of the Bible—He gives us examples and stories of ordinary people who by faith walked through doorways that led to change and even supernatural testimonies of God's power and plan for their life.

In the Book of Exodus, God opens a door for His people that will lead them out of bondage and into a place of freedom and promise. He uses the Hebrew word *bo*, which means to "exit," but it also means to "enter"; and it has so much more depth and promise. *Bo* can also mean the following:

> advance, apply, approach, arrive, associate, border, bring, bring to pass, come to pass, enter, enter and go, get, give, go, go through, harbor, harvest, indeed come, invade, keep on coming, present, proceed, reach, reenter, replace, return, set, spring, stand, sundown, sunset, sunrise, support, take, take place, visit, and so much more.

This small word, with such great weight and possibilities, is what the door that is opening in your life holds for you and your journey—endless possibilities.

We are going to look at the story of a family in the Old Testament who sensed God was doing something in their life in a difficult and fruitless season. We will unpack what was required of them and how they stepped into the threshold of a doorway. We will witness the powerful story of how an Ephesians 3:20 moment in their life unfolded—something more than they expected and beyond their comprehension.

In this verse, God says to His people, "When you come to the end of your thoughts and the end of your imagination, I start there." So if you are sensing God is doing something big in your life, something beyond your own abilities, then you are in the right place at the right time. You are getting ready to embrace the John 10:10 promise for your life, where the enemy of your destiny is silenced and the promise of purpose, provision, and prosperity is released. You are ready to walk through your *Door to More.*

"I am the door.
If anyone enters
by Me, he will
be saved, and
will go in and out
and find pasture."

—Jesus Christ

John 10:9

1

THE POWER OF A DOORWAY

Doorways—they're all around us. They're in our houses, schools, stores, workplaces, and churches. Each door is an opening or passageway allowing us to move from one place and enter another. Think about how many doorways you walk through every day. What might life be like without them?

Just as there are doorways in the natural, there are doorways in the spiritual realm. They allow you to move from one place to another—to exit one season and enter the next. They exist to transport you out of old places and into new places, moving you from one level of glory to another. When you come to a doorway, you are able to see things you've not seen before. On the other side of that threshold are opportunities for advancement, growth, and greater blessings than you've ever known. Indeed, doorways are powerful!

NOAH FOUND HIMSELF AT A DOORWAY.

God came to Noah and revealed that He was about to destroy the entire world by a Flood. Noah's doorway was the passage between the pre-Flood and post-Flood world, between judgment and grace. As he stood in the doorway, God allowed him to see what was coming and prepare himself and his family for life on the other side. He was given the assignment to build a boat of epic proportions.

There was a problem. Noah was building a boat, but there was no water to make it float. He was in a dry season. The fact is, no rain had ever fallen since the beginning of time, including the 600 years Noah had been alive. Nevertheless, he did not focus on what he could see. He focused on what God had said. Step by step, he followed God's blueprint, laboring faithfully with his three sons for over a century. He obeyed God completely and constructed an ark that would preserve not only his family but also a sampling of all the animals in the known world.

Do you feel like Noah? Are you in a dry season? Has God told you to do something that makes no sense? Have you obediently been walking out His plan, but you cannot see the fullness of what He has for you in the future? Rest assured, any time God gives you a vision for your life, there's always provision for your life. Whatever you need to live out your purpose and destiny will be provided, just as it was for Noah.

"In the six hundredth year of Noah's life, in the second month, the seventeenth day of the month, on that day all the fountains of the great deep were broken up, and the windows of heaven were opened" (Genesis 7:11). This was Noah's D-day—the day he walked through the doorway. What God had prepared and preserved since the beginning of time was released in that moment. Water came from above and from below. The unseen became seen. The impossible became possible. God provided water to float Noah's boat, and He's about to float your boat too!

DAVID FOUND HIMSELF AT A DOORWAY.

There he was . . . alone in the fields on the backside of nowhere. This ruddy, strapping young man was the youngest of eight. He had the responsibility of shepherding his father's sheep, and in the process he had fought and defeated a lion and a bear. Though highly skilled with a sling and a stone, he was equally accomplished as a songwriter and worshiper of God.

Then the day came—the day the great prophet came to his family's home. Samuel had seen all of Jesse's sons, but the Lord had not chosen any of them. Now he waited for the last one to arrive. "We will not sit down till he comes here," Samuel said (1 Samuel 16:11). Responding to his father's call to come in out of the fields, David arrived at his doorway to destiny. As he stood before the longhaired prophet, he was anointed with oil, "and the Spirit of the Lord came upon David from that day forward" (v. 13).

Just as Samuel refused to sit and rest until David arrived, your destiny will not rest until you walk into it. You will receive God's anointing and live out your purpose. The day David stood in the doorway and was anointed, everything changed. In an instant, he was catapulted from shepherd boy to king of Israel. Clearly, one doorway can change everything in your life.

DISCERN THE DOOR THAT IS BEFORE YOU.

As you go through life, you will find yourself standing before one of three types of doors: open doors, closed doors, or locked doors. Some doors are "God doors" He has destined you to walk through, and other doors are "trap doors" the enemy has arranged to pull you down into defeat. The key is to learn to discern which door is in front of you.

The good news is, God knows which doors you are to walk through and which doors you need to walk away from. He can see what's on the other side of every door, whether it will bring blessings or curses. As you stay close to Him, you will learn to discern which doors He is opening and which ones He is closing. The Bible says God has the "key in his hand, opening doors no one can lock, locking doors no one can open" (Revelation 3:7 TM).

Ultimately, with every door that is of God, *Jesus is the door.* In John 10:9 He said, "I am the door. If anyone enters by Me, he will be saved, and will go in and out and find pasture." In the very next verse, Jesus revealed what the door of His life leads to and what doors from the enemy produce. He said, "The thief does not come except to steal, and to kill, and to destroy. I have come that they may have life, and that they may have it more abundantly" (v. 10). God's doors bring salvation and advancement. They align you and connect you to Christ and the right people you need to help fulfill your purpose.

OPEN DOORS SOMETIMES BRING CHALLENGES.

While open doors are a wonderful blessing, they are sometimes accompanied with challenges. Take Paul's trip to Ephesus, for example. When writing to the believers at Corinth, he said, "I will stay in Ephesus until Pentecost, for a wide door for effective work has opened to me, and there are many adversaries" (1 Corinthians 16:8-9 ESV). God had clearly opened a door for the Gospel, and the enemy was not happy. Consequently, he stirred up a lot of trouble for Paul.

You need to know not every opportunity God brings your way will be met with clear sailing. You have an adversary that is very real, and he and his cohorts are not going to roll out the red carpet for you to accomplish God's plan. On the contrary, the devil will do his best to frustrate your efforts at every turn. He is out to steal, kill, and destroy.

In Acts 20:23-24a, Paul said, "The Holy Spirit testifies in every city, saying that chains and tribulations await me. But none of these things move me." Paul knew he was going to face troubles, but it didn't matter. Basically, his response to the enemy was, "Devil, I'm not impressed. I don't care what you try to throw in my path, you can't stop me. God's got my back regardless of your attack. I'm moving forward!" Paul refused to quit. God had infused him with a supernatural resolve to push back against the enemy, and He'll do the same for you if you'll ask Him.

SOMETIMES GOD *CLOSES* THE DOOR.

The Apostle Paul also experienced closed doors. During his second missionary journey, "Paul and Silas traveled through the area of Phrygia and Galatia, because the Holy Spirit had prevented them from preaching the word in the province of Asia at that time. Then coming to the borders of Mysia, they headed north for the province of Bithynia, but again the Spirit of Jesus did not allow them to go there" (Acts 16:6-7 NLT).

Get this: Paul had a word from God and was ready to preach, but the Spirit prevented him. He closed the door so the missionaries could not advance. God withdrew His peace and created a blockade of circumstances for Paul and his team because He saw things they could not see. The closed door was actually a blessing in disguise.

I love when God opens a door in my life. But there are also times when He closes a door. In the past,

I've tried to pry doors open—knock them down, and even bulldoze through them. Take it from me, this is one of the worst things you can do. Now if a door I wanted to walk through is closed, I've learned to step back and pray, "Holy Spirit, if You're closing this door, I honor Your decision and trust Your wisdom. Give me Your peace to wait for the open door You have ahead. I believe You know what's best."

SOMETIMES THE DOOR IS *LOCKED* FOR GOOD REASON.

There are also times when the door that's before us is a "God door," but it's locked. Have you encountered one of these? You knew it was something God was calling you to—a doorway to your destiny, filled with His purpose for your life, but it was locked. I've encountered this myself, and I've discovered if the door is locked, there is a good reason. In most cases, the timing is not right.

Paul encountered locked doors—doors he knew in his spirit were of God. How did he deal with them? He prayed and encouraged others to do the same. He told believers, "Pray for us, too, that *God may open a door* for our message, so that we may proclaim the mystery of Christ, for which I am in chains" (Colossians 4:3 NIV). Essentially Paul said, "I'm carrying the message of the Gospel, and I feel compelled to deliver it. But it's on lockdown until God opens the door. Pray for us that He will open a door at the right season for us to declare His truth."

The purpose and plan of God are powerful, but without the timing of God, your efforts will never be fruitful. If the door is locked and you believe it's one He wants you to walk through, hold steady. Don't try to finagle your way through it. Only one key is needed to unlock it, and God has it. The fact is, the key you need is likely the character you need to sustain you in your next season.

God is trying to build and develop something in you for what's ahead. Maybe you need greater faith, more self-control, or a greater understanding of your identity in Christ. Maybe God is preparing your spouse or family members. Whatever the case may be, you can know it is good and you will be glad you have what you need when the time comes.

Friend, trust God's timing. Don't get consumed by what you see in the natural. The difficulties and impossibilities you perceive can all be gone in an instant. You serve the God who opens doors no man can open and closes doors no man can close. If you're meant to walk through a door, it will open in the right way at the right time—God's time! More on this in our final chapter.

HOW SHOULD YOU RESPOND IN YOUR "MIDNIGHT HOUR"?

You might be in a very dark place as you read this chapter. It's possibly the darkest place you've ever been in your life. First, you need to know that there's nothing wrong with you, and God has not stopped loving you. All believers will encounter difficult trials and tribulations at times. Jesus made this fact clear (see John 16:33). But your midnight hour does not have to be the worst moment of your life. Instead, it can be the beginning of a brand new day.

Paul and Silas experienced a very difficult, dark time while ministering in the Macedonian city of Philippi. After leading Lydia and her family to the Lord and setting a slave girl free from an evil spirit, they were falsely accused of inciting a rebellion against the Roman government. The two men were then dragged into the town square, stripped of their clothes, beaten with rods, and thrown into the deepest part of the prison. By all appearances, things seemed hopeless.

It was now midnight, and Paul and Silas were locked in shackles. Things were looking grim. Then something happened—something unexpected and quite unusual. The Bible says, "at midnight Paul and Silas were praying and singing hymns to God, and the prisoners were listening to them" (Acts 16:25). I know of various things people do in their midnight hour. Some hide and some complain, while others rant and rave and blame God for their troubles. Not Paul and Silas. These two chose to pray and sing praise to God in the midst of their mess.

What resulted is nothing short of phenomenal. "Suddenly there was a great earthquake, so that the foundations of the prison were shaken; and immediately all the doors were opened and everyone's chains were loosed" (Acts 16:26). The moment the doors opened, their shackles began to fall off. You may be bound in certain areas of your life, but God wants you to know as you trust Him and praise Him in your midnight hour, He will intervene. Not only will He open the door to your new season, He will also set you *free* from what once had you bound!

In the middle of the mayhem, the jailer was jolted from his sleep. Seeing the prison doors opened, he assumed all the inmates had all escaped on his watch. Knowing the consequences for such negligence, he quickly drew his sword to end his life. "But Paul called with a loud voice, saying, 'Do yourself no harm, for we are all here.' Then he [the jailer] called for a light, ran in, and fell down trembling before Paul and Silas. And he brought them out and said, 'Sirs, what must I do to be saved?'" (Acts 16:28-30). Sometimes your open doors are not about you getting out; they're about who God wants to bring into your life. Such was the case with the jailer. Paul and Silas' praise in the midst of their brokenness opened the door for the jailer and his family to receive Christ as their Savior.

In their darkest hour, Paul and Silas worshiped God, and a revival hit the jailhouse! The Bible says the jailer and his entire household chose to believe in God and were baptized. The greatest way to see a door unlock in your life is to worship God in your midnight hour. While this includes singing and offering praise to God, it also means being obedient and doing the right thing in spite of the circumstances.

There's one more thing you need to see. When Paul and Silas walked out the door of the jailhouse and into the door of the warden's house, the jailer who put them in chains one day was the same one who washed their wounds and served them a meal the next day. Amazing! The things that beat you down and held you captive in your last season may be the very things that lift you up in your new season. Your testimony is being written, and it has victory all over it!

WHAT DO YOU SEE BEFORE YOU?

Are you standing before an open door? Walk through it. Are you standing before a closed door? Leave it alone. If the door is locked and you believe it is a God door, there is a reason. Be still and see what God has in store. Don't try to push your way through or make something happen on your own. *Wait.* "Those who wait upon God get fresh strength. They spread their wings and soar like eagles, they run and don't get tired, they walk and don't lag behind" (Isaiah 40:31 TM).

As you read through this book, I'm praying and believing God is going to bring alignment to your life. Alignment always precedes assignment. If you let Him, God will align you with His Word and His Spirit. He will put you on the same page with what He says in Scripture and what His Spirit is doing on earth. I call this *vertical connection.* He promises that as you "roll your works upon the Lord [commit and trust them wholly to Him; He will cause your thoughts to become agreeable to His will, and] so shall your plans be established and succeed" (Proverbs 16:3 AMPC).

The greater your vertical connection is, the greater your horizontal connection and impact will be. As God aligns you with His Word and His Spirit, He will also align you with the people, places, and things you need to fulfill the assignment on your life. Relationships are the currency of the Kingdom. Together we are better. We'll take a closer look at the supernatural strength of partnership in the pages ahead.

Friend, I truly believe God is preparing and positioning you for great things. It's no accident or coincidence that you're reading this book at this time. As you listen to Him and let Him lead, He's going to open the door to your next season. He's going to reignite your passion and reconnect you to your purpose and the intentional design He has for your life. New places with new faces await. Unexpected opportunities are coming. Get ready! One doorway can change everything in your life.

DISCOVERING YOUR DOORWAY

In light of what you just read about the *power of a doorway*, reflect on and respond to these personalized thoughts and questions.

• What is my **greatest takeaway** from this chapter? What is most important to me in this moment that I want to remember?

____

____

____

____

• I believe the **action steps** God is prompting me to take are:

____

____

____

____

• Take time to **pray**: "Lord, what are You doing in my life right now? What are You trying to teach me and build in me?"

Listen and *write* what He reveals. Ask Him to help you trust Him and praise Him, regardless of what you see or how you feel.

____

____

____

____

"The most holy and necessary practice in our spiritual life is the presence of God. That means finding constant pleasure in His divine company, speaking humbly and lovingly with Him in all seasons, at every moment, without limiting the conversation in any way."

—Brother Lawrence

The Practice of the Presence of God

2

HOW TO ATTRACT THE PRESENCE OF GOD

Can you think of someone you'd love to be around—someone whose *presence* is captivating, exciting, and exhilarating? Would it be a member of the royal family or the President of the United States? Would it be a highly successful sports hero or a charming, award-winning actor? How about a brilliant historian or an anointed Bible teacher? As wonderful and rewarding as being in the presence of these people may be, it is no match for the indescribable, awe-inspiring presence of God.

No one in the past, present, or future can compare with your Creator! He is all-knowing and all-powerful. He is incredibly loving, caring, and forgiving. He is matchless in mercy and patience and totally selfless in motive. Who is like Him? No one. And He longs to be in relationship with **you**! The Bible says, "The Holy Spirit whom God has placed within us, watches over us with tender jealousy" (James 4:5b TLB).

There's something amazing about experiencing the presence of God. Many have tasted of this privilege throughout history, including a notable woman who lived in the ancient city of Shunem during the time of the prophet Elisha.

ENTER THE SHUNAMMITE WOMAN.

The city of Shunem was located north of Samaria near the valley of Jezreel. That is where the Shunnamite woman lived. What's most interesting about her life is her interaction with Elisha, the mighty prophet of God—one of the most powerful men from Old Testament times. In those days, God's presence would rest on certain individuals for specific tasks. Elisha was one such person.

Elisha carried a double portion of the anointing that had rested on the prophet Elijah, the one who called fire down on Mount Carmel and heard the sound of an abundance of rain in a season of drought and famine. Elisha parted the waters of the Jordan River, blinded the eyes of the entire Aramean army, and raised a dead boy back to life. Elisha made an ax head float in water, cured Naaman of leprosy, and multiplied a widow's oil (a story we will examine fully in chapter 6). Without question, the presence of God rested heavily on Elisha. And here is where our story begins.

> Now it happened one day that Elisha went to Shunem, where there was a notable woman, and she persuaded him to eat some food. So it was, as

> often as he passed by, he would turn in there to eat some food. And she said to her husband, "Look now, I know that this is a holy man of God, who passes by us regularly. Please, let us make a small upper room on the wall; and let us put a bed for him there, and a table and a chair and a lampstand; so it will be, whenever he comes to us, he can turn in there."
>
> And it happened one day that he came there, and he turned in to the upper room and lay down there (2 Kings 4:8-11).

Notice what's written in verse 8. The Bible says this woman "persuaded him to eat some food." In other words, she "urged" Elisha to eat something (NIV). She invited him and convinced him to come to her home and enjoy a meal, and she succeeded in her efforts. Verse 8 confirms "as often as he passed by, that he turned in there to eat some food."

But why did the Shunammite woman go to such lengths to persuade Elisha to come to her home? The answer is in verse 9: "She said to her husband, 'I know that this man who often comes our way is a holy man of God" (NIV). This woman could see something was different about Elisha. He carried the presence of God with him in a way no one else did, and she was magnetically drawn to it. He was the prophet of power for that hour, and when he was around, things changed for the better.

Again and again, the Shunammite woman prepared and put out the best meals she could muster, effectively enticing the man of God to come. She liked what she experienced when Elisha was around and desired a deeper relationship with him. Obviously, what she was doing attracted Elisha's presence. As often as he passed by, he turned in there to eat some food. And by attracting Elisha's presence, she attracted God's presence. His anointing was regularly *in the house*—her house. The Shunammite woman learned how to attract the presence of God, and it opened a doorway of great blessing for her and her husband beyond their wildest dreams.

HOW ABOUT YOU?

Would you like to experience God's anointing regularly? Something tells me you just answered yes. Who wouldn't want to experience the all-knowing, all-powerful presence of God in their life? Deep inside every human heart, including yours, is an empty place longing to be filled with Him. The good news is, God's Word teaches you how. There are some specific things you can do to effectively attract the presence of God—things that will touch His heart and make Him want to move into your life.

There are eleven specific things in Scripture that will invite and persuade the Spirit of God to "turn in" and fellowship with you. These are attitudes and actions you can cultivate and put in to practice to enjoy God's presence and companionship.

1. *DESIRE* ATTRACTS GOD'S PRESENCE.

The Bible teaches when you have a desire to get close to God, He desires to get close to you. James 4:8 says, "Draw near to God and He will draw near to you." The more you press in and pursue God, the more you'll discover His goodness and the diverse depth of His character. There is no end to your learning and understanding.

Jesus spoke about the power of desire, saying, "Blessed are those who hunger and thirst for righteousness, for they shall be filled" (Matthew 5:6). When you are hungry for the things of God, He will personally see to it that your hunger is satisfied. *Desire* attracts God's presence.

2. *HUMILITY* ATTRACTS GOD'S PRESENCE.

Few things attract the presence of God more than humility. The psalmist David said God "does not forget the cry of the humble" (Psalm 9:12); He hears their desires (10:17). When you walk in humility, you attract God's goodness and grace to your life. Repeatedly, God says He resists and rejects the proud but gives grace to the humble (Proverbs 3:34; James 4:6; 1 Peter 5:5). While humility attracts God's presence, pride drives Him away.

There have been countless individuals, corporations, businesses, and ministries ruined because of pride. Indeed, "A man's pride will bring him low, but the humble in spirit will retain honor" (Proverbs 29:23). There is no faster route to promotion than humility.

Do you want to advance? "Humble yourselves in the sight of the Lord, and he will lift you up" (James 4:10). As you bow, He lifts. As you lower yourself in submission to Him, He will raise you up and exalt you. *Humility* attracts the presence of God.

3. *OBEDIENCE* ATTRACTS GOD'S PRESENCE.

Not only do humility and desire attract God's presence, obedience does as well. What's obedience? Doing what God said, plain and simple. He has called you to be obedient to what He has said in His Word and spoken directly to your heart. How important is obedience in God's eyes? The prophet Samuel said, "To obey is better than sacrifice" (1 Samuel 15:22).

"Noah did everything God commanded him" (Genesis 7:5). He totally obeyed. He built the ark exactly how God told him. He brought a pair of every known animal into the ark exactly as God said. Even though there was no water to be seen to float the boat God told him to build, Noah obeyed. Eventually the *vision* for his life was met with *provision* for his life. Because of Noah's obedience, God "remembered" him and his family and blessed them with new life in the new world (8:1).

What happens as you walk in obedience to the Word of God? You attract His presence. His Spirit is drawn to you, and "where the Spirit of the Lord is, there is freedom" (2 Corinthians 3:17 NIV). His presence empowers you to get up and make up your mind that what He's declared is already a done deal.

With confidence you can say, "Lord, I don't know how everything is going to work out, but I don't have to know. I just have to obey. I just have to walk out the steps You've given me. I am living by *Your* Word, not mine. And as I am "willing and obedient, [I] will eat the good things of the land" (Isaiah 1:19 NIV). *Obedience* attracts the presence of God.

4. *UNITY* ATTRACTS GOD'S PRESENCE.

Unity is powerful. When you're in unity with God and your brothers and sisters in the faith, you're walking in agreement. It is a spirit of oneness, and God loves it. Psalm 133:1, 3 says, "Behold, how good and how pleasant it is for brethren to dwell together in unity! . . . For there the Lord commanded the blessing—life forevermore." This means when God sees you walking in unity, He puts a bull's-eye on you at which He aims His blessings!

The opposite is also true. If you're walking in strife or disunity, the enemy puts a bull's-eye on you. "For where envy and self-seeking exist, confusion and every evil thing are there" (James 3:16). As a pastor, I tell our people, "citylife church is a place of *no drama.* We love God and we love people. We've made up our mind that we're not going to fight or complain. We're going to labor together and do the work of the Lord in the city of Tampa and the world." Pursuing and preserving unity has consistently attracted the presence of God to our church.

I challenge you to get up every day and say, "Lord, I *choose* to walk in unity with Your Word, Your Spirit, and the people You've placed around me. I'm not going to fight or feud with others. I may not always agree with them, but I can agreeably disagree. Please strengthen me by the power of Your Spirit." As you pursue unity, God puts a bull's-eye on you to receive His blessings! Unity attracts God's presence.

5. *BROKENNESS* ATTRACTS GOD'S PRESENCE.

Brokenness may not be something you've heard talked about in a positive light, but according to God's Word, it can be a good thing. "The Lord is close to the brokenhearted; he rescues those whose spirits are crushed" (Psalm 34:18 NLT). When you humble yourself and allow God to deal with the areas of your life that are not in unity with His Word, it attracts His presence. When you let Him break you and remold you into the image of Jesus, His Spirit is drawn to you.

David was a man after God's heart, but there were areas in his life that needed to be corrected. That's why He cried out, "Search me, O God, and know my heart; try me, and know my anxieties; and see if there is any wicked way in me, and lead me in the way everlasting" (Psalm 139:23-24). David's willingness to be broken and worked on by God won God's favor and attracted His presence. The same will happen for you. Brokenness attracts the presence of God.

6. *PRAYER* ATTRACTS GOD'S PRESENCE.

Did you know prayer attracts God's presence? It does. Prayer is two-way communication—your direct line and access to Heaven to offer God your petitions and hear Him speak to you. The only way you can go anywhere in the Kingdom is through prayer. It is the master key that opens new doors to new places God is calling you to walk.

The Bible teaches us to "pray without ceasing" (1 Thessalonians 5:17). This does not mean we're to walk around jibber-jabbering all day. It simply means our spirit is always open and in connection with God's Spirit. In this state of communion, He can easily speak a word of direction to us and we can easily speak to Him.

As you stay in communion with God through prayer, it lets Him know you deeply desire His presence in your life. It's like saying, "Lord, I need Your voice in my life! I want You to be with me not just on Sundays, but on Mondays, Tuesdays, Wednesdays, Thursdays, Fridays, and Saturdays." If you fail to talk and listen to God, You'll miss out on His plans and the blessings He has for your life.

If you think about it, prayer is like a superconductor of God's presence. It combines the attitude of *humility*, the action of *obedience*, and the condition of *brokenness*. Prayer also employs *faith*, *praise*, and *worship*, which we will explore shortly. God never wants you to be afraid to pray. In fact, He says to boldly walk into His presence and ask Him for whatever you need (see Hebrews 4:16).

With confidence you can pray, "Father, I need Your mercy and forgiveness for my mistakes. I need You to direct my path. I need Your anointing in my life because without it I'm weak and anemic. I need You to heal my marriage and touch my kids. I need You to bless my finances. You've been in my yesterday, and now I need You in my today and tomorrow. Thank You for loving me and wanting to be personally involved in my life. I love You, Lord, and I bless Your holy name."

Anytime and anywhere, you can pray about anything. Prayer attracts the presence of God.

7. *PRAISE* ATTRACTS GOD'S PRESENCE.

Something else that serves as a runway for God's presence to land is praise. Psalm 22:3 says, "You are holy, O You who inhabits the praises of Israel" (MEV). The word *inhabits* means "lives in" or "dwells." When you choose to praise God, He shows up and enthrones Himself on your praise. Every time you open your mouth and declare how good God is, He is drawn to you and His presence becomes more real. When He shows up, His grace shows up, and *everything* comes with His grace: His mercy, favor, peace, joy, encouragement, wisdom, direction, healing, and every other "good and perfect gift" you can imagine (James 1:27).

In out last chapter, we talked about Paul and Silas praising God in their midnight hour. God was so moved by what He heard, it was as if He started tapping His foot to the beat of their song. Suddenly, an earthquake shook the prison, and everyone's chains were loosed, the doors were opened, and the hearts of the jailer and his family became hungry for the Gospel.

When David rolled up on the scene in the valley of Elah and saw what was going on, the situation was bleak. All the mighty men, including King Saul, were hiding and overwhelmed with fear. For forty days and nights Goliath had taunted and intimidated the entire army of Israel, and not one man was willing to stand against the Philistine champion. What was David's response to the giant's blasphemous insults? Praise!

Turning to King Saul, David said, "The Lord, who delivered me from the paw of the lion and from the paw of the bear, He will deliver me from the hand of this Philistine" (1 Samuel 17:37). Can you hear the praise in David's voice? Basically, he said, "I serve a God who has shown up before, oh king. And I know He will show up again!"

After going down to the brook and retrieving five smooth stones to place in his pouch, David took to the battlefield to face Goliath. Again, he gave God praise, declaring to the giant, "I come to you in the name of the Lord of hosts, the God of the armies of Israel, whom you have defied. This day the Lord will deliver you into my hand . . . that all the earth may know that there is a God in Israel" (vv. 45-47). David knew in his heart, *As long as I am in communion with that name and I have praise in my mouth, giants have to fall!* The same is true for us. Praise attracts the presence of God.

8. *WORSHIP* ATTRACTS GOD'S PRESENCE.

It's been said that "worship is God's address," and that is true. When we worship from a sincere heart, we magnetically attract the presence of God. Where praise ends, worship begins. It is an even deeper expression of devotion and affection for God—an even greater level of surrender, expressing love, honor, and respect for Him.

It's important to realize worship is not just singing a song, taking a knee, raising your hands, or expressing yourself through dance. While all these things are part of worship and touch God's heart, worship is the way you live. It's a lifestyle, not merely a ceremony.

Worship is getting up every day and raising your children in the right way. It's going to work and operating in honesty and integrity, honoring your boss and using your gifts with excellence. Worship is hearing the Word of God and obediently living it out. It's being a good steward of your finances and your time. It's putting one foot in front of the other every day and choosing to do the right thing, regardless of what others think or the consequences it may bring. Worship is a lifestyle! Worship attracts God's presence.

9. *GENEROSITY* ATTRACTS GOD'S PRESENCE.

Generosity is a Kingdom attribute that causes God to move into your life in a greater way. To be generous is to be like God. The Bible says, "God so loved the world that He *gave* His only begotten Son . . . " (John 3:16). God is the greatest Giver the world will ever know, and when you're generous you imitate Him.

Being generous means you're a good steward of what God has given you. You focus on others more and more, looking for ways to be a blessing with your time, your talent, and your treasure. You allow God to use you to *be* a blessing and not just *receive* a blessing. When God called Abraham, He said, "I will bless you and make your name great; and you shall be a blessing" (Genesis 12:2). The Bible teaches, "If you are Christ's, then you are Abraham's seed, and heirs according to the promise" (Galatians 3:29). In other words, what God spoke to Abraham He has also spoken to you: "I will bless you, and you shall be a blessing!"

"So then . . . let us do good [morally] to all people. . . . Be mindful to be a blessing, especially to those of the household of faith [those who belong to God's family with you, the believers]" (Galatians 6:10 AMPC). Generosity attracts the presence of God.

10. *PREPARATION* ATTRACTS GOD'S PRESENCE.

Preparation is a *must* to succeed. What is preparation? It is allowing God to mold and shape us into the person of Jesus. It is cooperating with His Spirit and allowing His Word to define and refine who we are. This attracts God's presence, making Him want to be near us. The Bible says He is the Potter and we are the clay (Jeremiah 18:3-6). When we flow with the process of preparation, we allow His character to take root in our life.

Nothing of lasting value happens without preparation. No NFL team has ever won a championship without the preparation of the preseason and regular practices throughout the season. No orchestra gives a flawless performance without scores of rehearsals. And no doctor conducts brain surgery without countless hours of study, in-depth training, and hands-on residency. Preparation is a must to succeed.

God can never work *through* you unless He first works *on* you and *in* you. Instead of worrying about those around you and the issues *they* need to deal with, look in the mirror and say, "Father, please work in my life and change me. I will not run from preparation—I will embrace it. I will no longer dread the process. Instead, I'm excited about what You're doing and what You're going to do!" As you cultivate a contrite spirit—one that's willing to be molded and shaped into a "vessel of honor"—you will be prepared for His service (2 Timothy 2:20-22). Preparation attracts God's presence.

11. *FAITH* ATTRACTS GOD'S PRESENCE.

Faith is the fuel of the Kingdom. "What is faith? It is the confident assurance that something we want is going to happen. It is the certainty that what we hope for is waiting for us, even though we cannot see it up ahead" (Hebrews 11:1 TLB). When you walk by faith, you are saying, "God, I trust You and want to please You. I'm going to be obedient to Your Word regardless of what things look like, what others say, or how I feel. You are God, and You know what's best."

The Bible says, "No one can please God without faith" (Hebrews 11:6a GW). Therefore, when you live by faith, you are pleasing God. Faith cooperates and allows the preparation process to begin and continue in your life. This means you believe God is at work in you and around you, causing all things to work together for your good because you love Him and He has purpose for your life (see Romans 8:28). Indeed, faith attracts the presence of God.

REMEMBER THE SHUNAMMITE WOMAN?

As we began the chapter, we learned about the notable woman from Shunem who was hungry for the presence of God she saw in Elisha. She was so hungry that she began to prepare and put out food to persuade him to stop in and stay with her and her husband. And it worked. "So it was, as often as he passed by, he would turn in there to eat some food" (2 Kings 4:8b). The Shunammite woman's actions launched her on a journey that would take her to the doorway of a new season—a season of blessing so great she never thought was possible.

There are places God desires to take you—places marked by blessings so great you never dreamed were possible. But you'll never reach or walk through the doorway to your destiny without the presence of God in your life. Moses understood God's presence was indispensable. He knew he and the people of Israel desperately needed God as they journeyed to the Promised Land. That's why he said, "If Your Presence does not go with us, do not bring us up from here" (Exodus 33:15).

The Shunammite woman and her husband successfully attracted the presence of God. Not only did Elisha stop in occasionally, he also began to stay with them for longer periods of time. He was so blessed by their attentive care that there came a point when he called for them to come to him so he could speak a blessing over their lives.

"Get ready!" Elisha said. "About this time next year, the impossible will become possible! The season you're about to enter will look nothing like one you're in now. Your future looks better than your present. Get ready!"

"TURN IN HERE, LORD!"

God is always on the move. He's always looking for those He can bless. "For the eyes of the Lord run to and fro throughout the whole earth, to show Himself strong on behalf of those whose heart is loyal to Him" (2 Chronicles 16:9). The question is, are *you* a person He turns in to visit? Are you someone purposely attracting His presence? Are you a target for His blessings?

My heart's cry is, "God, I know You're moving on the earth. Please, turn in here! Move into my life! Move into the Stewart house! Move into citylife church! Without Your presence, we can do nothing. Our natural only becomes supernatural if You're abiding with us. Your presence is the game-changer. With You in our life, mountains begin to move, armies are defeated, giants begin to fall! Oh, Lord, **turn in here**!"

Is that your heart's cry? Then begin to put into practice the things that attract God's presence. Begin to develop a *desire* for Him above everything else. Walk *humbly* before Him, *obeying* His Word and the promptings of His Spirit. Choose to pursue *unity* with Him and others. Allow God to *break* you where you need to be broken. Cooperate with the process of *preparation* He has planned for your life. Through *prayer*, keep the lines of communication and communion open. Become a person of *praise* and *worship*, expressing your love and devotion to Him more and more. Be *generous*, not stingy, with your time, talent, and treasure as He is generous with you. Live by *faith* moment by moment, day by day. As you live like this, God is overwhelmingly attracted to you!

There's a doorway in your future.

God is drawing you to it.

You won't be disappointed!

DISCOVERING YOUR DOORWAY

• In light of what you just read about *attracting the presence of God*, reflect on and respond to these personalized thoughts and questions.

• What is my **greatest takeaway** from this chapter? What is most important to me in this moment that I want to remember?

____

____

____

• I believe the **action steps** God is prompting me to take are:

____

____

____

• Take time to **pray**: "Lord, thank You for longing to be in relationship with me. Thank You for showing me what attracts Your presence. What am I currently doing that persuades You to want to turn in and fellowship with me? In what areas can I come up higher?"

Listen and *write* what He reveals. Ask Him to help you trust Him and put into practice the things that attract His presence.

____

____

____

NOTES

"I liken the heart of man to a painter's canvas. What a man dreams and envisions is the paint. If the Christian takes the brush of faith and begins to paint on the canvas of his heart the pictures that God has revealed to him, those revelations become reality."

—Dr. Paul Yonggi Cho

The Fourth Dimension, Volume Two

3

CAN YOU SEE IT?

Perception is powerful. It's the way you see things—your awareness, your view—your insight into situations and circumstances and life itself. Your perception greatly influences how you think, how you speak, and ultimately how you act. It will either paralyze you or propel you. It can fill your heart with fear or great anticipation of something amazing just around the bend. That's why it is so important to periodically pause and ask yourself, *How am I seeing things?*

The truth is, there's more to life than meets the eye. Beyond the natural is the *super*natural—a dimension of the spirit that is far more real than what you can see. You can have perfect 20/20 vision in the natural but be totally blind in the spirit. Perception is the eye of the spirit. It is seeing the way God sees. Only He can open your eyes and give you the ability to see as He sees. That's what He did for the notable woman from Shunem. Let's look once again at this remarkable story.

PERCEPTION IS THE EYE OF THE SPIRIT.

> Now it happened one day that Elisha went to Shunem, where there was a notable woman, and she persuaded him to eat some food. So it was, as often as he passed by, he would turn in there to eat some food. And she said to her husband, "Look now, I know that this is a holy man of God, who passes by regularly. Please, let us make a small upper room on the wall; and let us put a bed for him there, and a table and a chair and a lampstand; so it will be, whenever he comes to us, he can turn in there."
>
> And it happened one day that he came there, and he turned in to the upper room and lay down there (2 Kings 4:8-11).

As we discovered in the last chapter, the Shunammite woman was drawn to the presence of God that rested heavily upon Elisha. When he was around, great things happened. Therefore, she began to prepare enticing meals to persuade him to stop in and stay with her and her husband. Her efforts were successful. And every time Elisha's presence was in the house, God's presence was in the house.

Then something shifted inside of her—something life-changing. Verse 9 says, "And she said to her husband, Behold now, I *perceive* that this is a holy man of God who passes by continually" (AMPC). As God's presence was in the house, the Shunammite's spirit was opened. She began to *see* something through the eye of her spirit. Not only did she perceive the presence of God on Elisha, she also got a prophetic glimpse of the possibilities ahead for her and her husband.

Something is happening in this house, she thought. *I don't know exactly what it is, but I sense something big is about to take place. And I don't want to miss it!*

Now this woman and her husband, as well as all who were living in the region, had just come out of a season of famine. Times had been tough. Yet on the heels of famine, Elisha began to travel within the region, and the Shunammite woman made meals for the man of God. Again and again, her heart was stirred when Elisha was present, and she began to *perceive* her future through the eye of her spirit.

Perhaps you have recently weathered a storm of hurricane proportions. The struggles you and your family have endured have taken their toll on you in many ways. Yet you perceive something is happening in your spirit. You don't know exactly what it is, but you sense God is about to do something new. Something better is coming for you and your family—something amazing.

I love the way God describes perception in First Corinthians 2:9-10 (NLT):

> No eye has seen, no ear has heard, and no mind has imagined what God has prepared for those who love him. But it was to us that God revealed these things by His Spirit. For his Spirit searches out everything and shows us even God's deep secrets.

Basically, God is saying through Paul, "I have things prepared for you beyond what you have seen, beyond what you have heard, and beyond what your mind has imagined. In fact, they are too BIG for you to comprehend on your own. But as you walk with Me and welcome My presence, I will reveal these things to you by My Spirit."

ANTICIPATE COMING ATTRACTIONS.

Perception—seeing with the eye of your spirit what God sees—is a gift of discernment. It's seeing beyond the pictures of your checkered past and messed-up present to a phenomenal future that is yet to come. God is not limited by time or space. In fact, while He's walking you through your crazy present, He's already in your future waiting for you to arrive. As you walk with Him and rest in His presence, He'll give you the ability to see as He sees.

If you think about it, perception is a lot like what happens when you go to the movies. Before the main feature, they play a reel of *coming attractions*. These are previews of upcoming movies producers want you to see. Seasoned professionals splice together some of each movie's hottest scenes to create a craving within you. These clips are breathtaking, gripping, and suspenseful. They leave you hanging on the edge of your seat wanting more. It's all done in hopes that you'll drop another $89 on two tickets, two popcorns, two drinks, and a jumbo box of candy. The preview pulls you in. You don't want to wait till it comes out on streaming to rent. It's so intriguing, you want to see it *now*!

In a way, that's what the gift of perception provides. It's a preview of what is to come. God, by His Spirit, reveals bits and pieces of your next season. He never shows you the whole movie all at once—only a snapshot. But the snapshot is so good you can't wait to see the full picture play out. God's preview of what is to come pulls you in and helps you believe your best is yet to come. Your new season will be far greater than your former season.

PREVIEW THE BREAKTHROUGH.

The woman from Shunem had successfully attracted Elisha to her home. The presence of God was in the house. The man of God was so touched by her attentive care that he called for her to speak a blessing over her life.

> Then he said to Gehazi his servant, "Call this Shunammite woman." When he had called her, she stood before him. And he said to him, "Say now to her, 'Look, you have been concerned for us with all this care. What can I do for you? Do you want me to speak on your behalf to the king or to the commander of the army?'" And she answered, "I dwell among my own people" (2 Kings 4:12-13).

Elisha saw the selfless acts of the Shunammite woman and was moved to action. *The Message* paraphrase of verse 13 says: "Through Gehazi, Elisha said, 'You've gone far beyond the call of duty in taking care of us; what can we do for you? Do you have a request we can bring to the king or to the commander of the army?' She replied, 'Nothing. I'm secure and satisfied in my family.'"

It's almost as if Elisha asked her, "Can we speak to the king or the commander of the army on your behalf? We've heard about a new subdivision that's going up on the other side of town. It's a beautiful gated community with a pool, country club, and a superb view. We've got an inside track and can get you in on the ground floor. What do you say?"

"I dwell among my own people," the Shunammite woman answered. In other words, "No, we don't need any special favors. We believe God is about to do something right here." This woman had a snapshot in her spirit—a preview of the breakthrough that was coming. And it would take place in *her home* and among *her family*. She didn't know all the details, but she was filled with expectancy. Basically, what she told Elisha communicated, "We're not looking to move. We're staying put. We believing God is going to bless us right here."

THIS TIME NEXT YEAR, THE MIRACLE WILL HAPPEN.

It's been said no one can out-give God, and this situation with the Shunammite woman confirms it. Elisha, the man of God acting on God's behalf, would not take no for an answer. Determined to bless this generous, selfless woman and her husband, he turned to his servant and said,

> "What then is to be done for her?" And Gehazi answered, "Actually, she has no son, and her

> husband is old." So he said, "Call her." When he had called her, she stood in the doorway. Then he said, "About this time next year you shall embrace a son" (2 Kings 4:14-16a).

I love this passage because it shows God's deep desire to bless us and His persistence to make it happen. I also love the phrase the Holy Spirit chose to use: "she stood in the doorway." This was not just any doorway. This was the doorway to her destiny. Once she stepped into the doorway and heard the details of what was coming, her life was forever changed. She had a clearer picture of God's best, and she would not settle for anything less.

Friend, if you can begin to perceive what God has planned for you—if you can get into His presence and see yourself in the next season He's prepared—it will astonish you. Is it possible to get a glimpse of what God is up to? Absolutely!

First Chronicles 12:32 tells us about "the sons of Issachar." Issachar was one of Jacob's twelve sons, so the sons of Issachar were his family line. They had a unique gift with which they served their family. The Bible says they had "understanding" of the times in which they lived.

Just like many trackers and explorers can anticipate and interpret certain natural events, the sons of Issachar were able to instinctively see things with the eye of their spirit. They were able to take into account where they had been, where they were presently, and determine the best course of action to move forward. This same gift of discernment is something God wants to give to us (see 2 Corinthians 12:10).

David wrote, "The steps of a [good] man are directed and established by the Lord when He delights in his way [and He busies Himself with his every step]" (Psalm 37:23 AMPC). Right now God is preparing you for what He has prepared for you, and He is directing your every step. So seek His presence. Don't settle for second best. Don't be content with good when God has great. The Shunammite woman didn't settle for second-rate—she got God's best. And so can you.

NOTHING IS IMPOSSIBLE WITH GOD.

Once Elisha delivered the sneak peek of what was coming, the Shunammite responded. "No, my lord. Man of God, do not lie to your maidservant!" (2 Kings 4:16). Basically, she looked at him and said, "Have you seen me? Have you seen my husband? We're old! Every time I look in the mirror and look at my husband, I'm reminded of the fact that it's too late for us to have children."

In *The Message*, this verse reads, "'O my master, O Holy Man,' she said, 'don't play games with me, teasing me with such fantasies!'" The preview she received was too good to be true.

There's just no way, she probably thought. *I knew something good was coming. I knew in my heart it would be special, but not* this special.

But it wasn't too good to be true. God makes the impossible possible! "By his mighty power at work within us [God] is able to do far more than we would ever dare to ask or even dream of—infinitely beyond our highest prayers, desires, thoughts, or hopes" (Ephesians 3:20 TLB). "For with God nothing is ever impossible and no word from God shall be without power or impossible of fulfillment" (Luke 1:37 AMPC).

When Elisha said, "About this time next year you shall embrace a son" (2 Kings 4:16), essentially he was saying, "This old house is about to be filled with new life!" Like the Shunammite woman and her husband, you may be past the age of producing on your own what God has spoken. They could not make things happen in their own strength, and neither can you. But God will show up on your behalf! He will make a way where there seems to be no way. Jesus said, "With men this is impossible, but with God all things are possible" (Matthew 19:26).

I CAN PERSONALLY IDENTIFY WITH THE SHUNAMMITE WOMAN.

Over fourteen years ago, my wife, Kaci, and I packed up what few belongings we had and moved to Tampa, Florida. Our two girls were three years old and three months old at the time. We became the lead pastors at a church that was almost ninety years old. It was filled with several hundred beautiful people, and they were gracious in welcoming us. But the experience was quite different than we expected.

In our season prior to Tampa, Kaci and I had replanted a church in Naples, Florida—starting that journey with about thirty people. We personally knew just about everyone, and they knew us because we had all grown up together. So when we arrived in Tampa, there was a major time of stretching that took place in us and in the congregation. All of us were trying to adjust, and at times it was very uncomfortable.

After being in the position about three months, I remember feeling like a square peg in a round hole. As Kaci and I sat in our living room, my mind began racing.

Did we make the right decision? I wondered. *Lord, we heard You speak. We believe You moved us here. But we just don't seem to fit here. What's going on?*

Thankfully, God had placed some friends and mentors around us to reaffirm and encourage us. One afternoon we felt so overwhelmed and discouraged as we sat in our family room flipping through television channels. I stopped on a Christian station where a pastor was being interviewed. I didn't know of him at the time, but he said something life-changing. His name was Bishop Paul Morton, and he was pastoring the Greater St. Stephens Church in New Orleans, Louisiana.

"In a moment, everything we had was destroyed," Pastor Morton said. "When Hurricane Katrina hit and the levees broke, water inundated our church in the lower ninth ward, and people from our congregation were thrust out all over the city. When the waters finally receded enough for us to get inside, the building was in total devastation."

At that point, I was glued to Bishop Morton, hanging on his every word. He continued.

"As I walked up the church steps with the murky water still lingering in the streets, I was broken. Yet in that moment, I sensed God was about to do something new." Then he began to sing: "Lord, whatever You're doing in this season, please don't do it without me."

Pastor Morton's testimony breathed new hope into me for what Kaci and I were feeling and facing. Suddenly, I began to perceive God had bigger and better plans ahead for our future. Within the next few months, He began to shake and shift things in our church, moving some people out and moving other people in. Once we were in alignment, His assignment became clear and took on divine momentum. What God has done and is doing since those early days is nothing short of miraculous!

WHAT DO YOU SEE?

Friend, God has something greater in your future. I don't know where you are or what you've been through, but God does. It may be that He took you out of one job to bring you into a better one. He may have moved you out of one city and relocated you to another in preparation for what He has planned. He may have disconnected you from one group of people so He can connect you in partnership with others. Yes, you may have felt abandoned, but your tomorrow is *abundant*! Yes, you may have felt awkward, but your future is *awesome*!

The things you've had to walk through, fight through, and wait through all have purpose. By faith, I dare you to say, "Lord, whatever You're doing in this season, please don't do it without me!" My prayer for you as you finish this chapter is for God to give you a preview of coming attractions—a snapshot of the great things He has prepared for your life. While He won't show you the whole movie, He'll give you the glimpse you need to pull you in and help you believe your best is yet to come.

In this moment—as you are reading this sentence—I believe God is saying to you, "Forget the former things; do not dwell on the past. See, I am doing a new thing! Now it springs up; do you not *perceive* it? I am making a way in the desert and streams in the wasteland" (Isaiah 43:18-19 NIV 1984). The Great I Am is at work right now on your behalf! He is busily working behind the scenes to put everything in place for what He has planned. He's about to take you and your family to places you've never been. Get ready!

DISCOVERING YOUR DOORWAY

Now that you've read the chapter "Can You See It?", take time to reflect on and respond to these personalized thoughts and questions.

• What is my **greatest takeaway** from this chapter? What is most important to me in this moment that I want to remember?

____
____
____
____

• I believe the **action steps** God is prompting me to take are:

____
____
____
____

• Take time to **pray**: "Lord, renew my perception. If there's anything I'm seeing incorrectly, please adjust my vision. Give me eyes to see the way You see. Give me the preview I need right now at the age and stage of life I am in, and give me the grace to trust You through the difficulties I'm facing. As You showed up for the Shunammite woman, show up for me. In Jesus' name."

Listen and *write* what He reveals.

____
____
____
____

*"Two are better than one,
and more happy jointly
than either of them could be
separately, more pleased in
one another than they
could be in themselves only,
mutually serviceable to
each other's welfare, and by
a united strength more
likely to do good to others."*

—Matthew Henry

The Matthew Henry Study Bible

4

THE POWER OF PARTNERSHIP

Batman had Robin. Sherlock Holmes had Dr. Watson. And Han Solo had Chewbacca. What do these dynamic duos all have in common? One thing—*partnership*. By Webster's definition, *partnership* is "the association of two or more persons for the purpose of undertaking and effectively accomplishing a common goal." Everybody needs somebody in their life. You will never fulfill your Kingdom assignment without the help of others.

FROM THE BEGINNING OF GOD'S WORD AND THROUGHOUT ITS PAGES . . .

God established the power of partnership and commands His blessing on it (see Psalm 133). For Adam He created Eve, declaring, "It is not good that man should be alone; I will make him a helper comparable to him" (Genesis 2:18). Eve was created to reign side-by-side with Adam—not over him or under him. God placed them in the Garden of Eden—together. He gave them dominion over everything—together.

God partnered Sarah with Abraham to be the father and mother to a generation of faith. To Moses He brought Aaron and eventually Joshua to help bring the Israelites out of bondage and into the Promised Land. For David, God raised up Johnathan to help him learn what he needed to learn before taking his rightful place on the throne. And for Elijah He raised up Elisha to be his apprentice and eventually continue his mission once he was taken from the earth.

Even Jesus, the Son of God who had all power in Heaven and earth, chose to partner with others to establish His kingdom. He could have founded His kingdom on His own, but He did not. Instead, He prayerfully and carefully picked twelve men to do life with for His three and a half years of ministry. Three of them became His closest companions—Peter, James, and John. With the twelve He selected sixty others—for a total of seventy-two—and together they turned the world right-side up for God's glory.

The woman from Shunem also had a partner—her husband. He played a vital role in bringing God's presence into their house and in seeing God's promised blessing become a reality in their lives. Let's continue learning from this extraordinary story.

THE SHUNAMMITE WOMAN WAS IN PARTNERSHIP WITH HER HUSBAND.

> And she said to her husband, "Look now, I know that this is a holy man of God, who passes by us regularly. Please, let us make a small upper room

> on the wall; and let us put a bed for him there, and a table and a chair and a lampstand; so it will be, whenever he comes to us, he can turn in there."
>
> And it happened one day that he came there, and he turned in to the upper room and lay down there (2 Kings 4:9-11).

Once the Shunammite woman perceived the presence of God on Elisha and successfully began to attract His presence into her home, she also got a prophetic glimpse of the possibilities ahead for her and her husband. With her perception and expectancy now expanded, she turned to her husband and basically said, "Let's work together to build a room for this man of God. Let's furnish it with a bed, a table, a chair, and a lampstand. God has given me a vision. He has stirred my heart to believe something greater is in our future, but my gifting alone will never accomplish it. I need you as my partner."

The Scriptures are silent on the specific details, but at some point between verses 10 and 11, the Shunammite woman's husband agreed to partner with her. Together, they combined their gifts and resources and did a makeover on their home. Through partnership, they expanded their capacity to house the presence of God by making a fully furnished guestroom for Elisha. The place and space was so inviting that he moved in and began to dwell in their home regularly. The partnership between the Shunammite woman and her husband produced positive results, and the best was yet to come.

PARTNERING WITH THE WRONG PEOPLE CAN BE DEVASTATING.

The Bible does not just give us examples of keeping company with the right people. It also shows us the devastation of being in partnership with the wrong people. One of the saddest examples of this is Sampson's decision to partner with Delilah. She was a Philistine, Israel's arch enemy. Sampson was looking for love in all the wrong places, and his unbridled lust lured him into a relationship that would cost him his life.

Once Sampson was smitten by Delilah's beauty, she took full advantage of the situation. Having been bribed by the Philistine rulers with a small fortune to get Sampson to reveal the mystery of his strength, she pestered him until he divulged his secret. The bottom line: Sampson's partnership with Delilah left him bald, blind, and weak. Although he killed more of his enemies at the time of his death than while he was alive, his life was snuffed out prematurely. What a sobering warning to the deadliness of wrong relationships!

The Bible says, "Do not be misled: 'Bad company corrupts good character'" (1 Corinthians 15:33 NIV). It also warns, "Make no friendship with an angry man, and with a furious man do not go, lest you learn his ways and set a snare for your soul" (Proverbs 22:24-25). Again and again, God cautions not to partner with those who are greedy, sexually immoral, slanderers, drunkards, or swindlers (see 1 Corinthians 5:11; Ephesians 5:3-7). Please hear me. The right people will propel you; the wrong people will derail you. If you partner with the wrong people, they will set you up for failure and set you back on your journey. They will delay and possibly derail you from your destiny. Be advised.

PARTNERING WITH THE RIGHT PEOPLE IS LIFE-GIVING.

On the other hand, having the right people in your life can propel you toward your purpose. They will promote you, push you forward, and cheer you on. They will look at you and say, "Better days are ahead! There are greater things in your future!" The right people will stretch you and bring out the character of God in you.

Being connected with the right people also increases your effectiveness. They expand your level of influence and multiply your impact. The right people in the right place at the right time allows for *synergy* to take place. *Synergy* simply means "the whole is greater than the one." God has called us to walk as a united force in the earth, and when we do, we exponentially multiply each other's effectiveness. I have personally seen this in my life.

Each Sunday as I minister, there are people I'm in partnership with who help me accomplish the call of God on my life. For instance, people serve as greeters in our parking lot and our lobby; we have people operating cameras and we have teachers and singers. I'm also blessed with amazing people who love to drive and help me get from one campus to the next. While en route, I am able to prep for what's ahead or simply take a breather. Every individual partnering with me and citylife church are so vital to help us fulfil our assignment. And as others are helping me, I'm helping them—giving them opportunities to use and grow their gifts. You would be amazed at what God will do through you when the right people are around you.

God's Word says, "Two can accomplish more than twice as much as one, for the results can be much better. If one falls, the other pulls him up; but if a man falls when he is alone, he's in trouble. And one standing alone can be attacked and defeated, but two can stand back-to-back and conquer; three is even better, for a triple-braided cord is not easily broken" (Ecclesiastes 4:9-10, 12 TLB). While one person can put a thousand enemies to flight, two can put ten thousand on the run when God is included (see Deuteronomy 32:30-31).

Through partnership God establishes something in our lives that the enemy cannot break.

GREATNESS HAPPENS WHEN YOU'RE ON THE SAME PAGE.

I have discovered our ministry is strongest and most effective when my wife, Kaci, and I are on the same page. The truth is, we are two opposite people. God has given her strengths I don't have, and He's given me strengths she doesn't have. When we collaborate as one and allow the gifts He's placed in each of us to work through us, we're at our greatest strength! Her strengths strengthen my weaknesses, and my strengths strengthen her weaknesses.

Yes, there have been seasons when Kaci and I were not on the same page. The busyness of life crept in and began to cripple our creativity. She was running here, and I was running there. We were moving at 100 mph in opposite directions, and things began to rattle as we were worn to a frazzle. But when we realized what was happening and pressed pause on life, we were able to reconnect and get back into alignment with God and each other. Some of the best times of discovering God's plan for our life together have been over breakfast at a favorite restaurant. In moments like these—sitting, talking, and listening to each other—divine destiny has been birthed.

Several years ago our church bought an old grocery store with the purpose of turning it in to our new house of worship. Amazingly, God allowed me to see in my spirit almost the entire layout of the building before one nail was driven. I saw the sanctuary, the offices, the parking lot—everything. I was able to sketch it all out on a piece of scrap paper. I took it to the architect, and he used it to draw the plans. Having creative vision is part of the gifting God has placed on my life.

Once the designer began drawing the plans, Kaci stepped in and began adding in the details. "We can put the coffee shop right here," she said, "and we can go with this kind of carpet on the floors and use these colors for the walls." That is part of her gifting. She loves to decorate and create and is great at it. I am not—trust me. There were times when she was picking things out, and I thought, *Oh, man, I don't know how those combinations are going to go together.* But once it was completed, everything came together and looked fabulous.

What happened? We were on the same page! Her gifts came together with my gifts. Her strengths came together with my strengths, and we complemented each other. What was once an old grocery store has now become a thriving house of worship! That's the supernatural strength of partnership. God puts us together with others so we become one in heart, one in vision, one in purpose. When we're on the same page, greatness happens.

WHAT'S KEEPING YOU FROM PARTNERING WITH OTHERS?

Probably the biggest reason people don't reach out and partner with others is because they've been hurt. Maybe that's you. Maybe you're reading this and thinking, *Tony, I've tried working with others, and I got burned. People I thought were my friends really let me down. I'm wounded, and I don't want to be hurt again.* If that's you, I understand. I've been hurt before too. It happens. None of us are perfect, and sometimes we hurt each other.

The truth is, we're human and we all make mistakes and poor choices at times. We have all wounded others and let them down. I've done it and you've done it. I've even done things at times that offended God. But with each situation, I've gone to Him. First, I've asked Him to forgive me, and He has—He always does (see 1 John 1:9). And if I hurt someone, I went and apologized and asked them to forgive me.

My point is, if you're hurt, *don't stay hurt.* Get healed. Give your hurt to God and choose to forgive. He will help you (see Philippians 4:13; James 4:6). No, they may never apologize, but that's okay. You don't need their apology to forgive. Ask God for strength to release them like He released you from your offenses, and move on. I can look back at where I've been and remember how God has forgiven me, and thus I can release those who have hurt me. By His grace I can begin to trust and partner with others again, and so can you.

Don't believe the lie that you can do life alone. You can't. You need other people.

GET TO KNOW THE PEOPLE YOU'RE RUNNING WITH.

At the 2008 Olympics in Beijing, China, the American women's 400-meter relay team was aiming to win the gold medal. When the day of their qualifying race finally arrived and the starting gun sounded, the unexpected happened. The worst sound a relay runner will ever hear was heard. On the last leg of the race, the runner missed the handoff and dropped the baton. It was devastating. Incredibly, just thirty minutes before, the American men's 400-meter relay team had botched the baton handoff in their race too.

The U.S. Olympic Committee was so overwhelmed by what happened, they brought in specialists and conducted an in-depth study on handing off the baton. They concluded it did not matter how gifted and talented the individual runners were. If there was not a partnership between the runners, the race would be lost every time.

For four years, they studied and worked diligently on the handoff. Relay runners trained to run, but the handoff became top priority. The 2012 Olympics in London rolled around, and the word was that the American women's 400-meter relay team had blazing speed and were ready to run. And run they did, without the baton being dropped. Each runner executed the handoff with precision timing. Not only did the U.S. women's team win the gold, they also set a world record.

While each individual runner was highly gifted, they were only as gifted as the persons to whom they were connected. You may be highly gifted and called by God to do great things. But unless you're in partnership with the right people, you will not accomplish your calling. You will not win your race. You will not be who God has called you to be. You need to humble yourself before Him and others. Pray for and look for His divine connections. As God brings them, turn to them and say, "I need you in my life. Your gifts complement me and will help me build for the next season, and mine will help you. Let's be partners."

God is building a doorway to your tomorrow. You will never get to it or through it by yourself. You need others. Be open and willing. Partner with the people God sends you, and they'll help you reach and fulfill your destiny.

PARTNERSHIP BUILDS A DOORWAY TO A NEW DIMENSION.

The Shunammite woman perceived God was moving and wanting to do something greater. Through the eye of the spirit, she was able to see beyond the now—beyond their current situation, beyond past hurts and disappointments, and beyond their former season of famine. She reached out to her husband and said, "I have a vision of God moving in our lives, and I want to make room for Him. My dream is to build Elisha a fully furnished place to stay. I can see it finished, but I need your gifts to make it a reality. Will you partner with me?"

The Shunammite's husband was the spiritual authority of that house, and she knew she needed to humbly submit to and work with him. God never operates outside of the spiritual authority He has established.

Her husband accepted the invitation, and together they began to build and furnish a room for the man of God. Once it was complete, Elisha began to dwell with them, and the longer he was there, the more the house changed. As he continued to observe the woman's selfless acts of kindness, the Spirit of God moved him to action.

> Through Gehazi, Elisha said, "You've gone far beyond the call of duty in taking care of us; what can we do for you? Do you have a request we can bring to the king or to the commander of the army?" She replied, "Nothing. I'm secure and satisfied in my family" (2 Kings 4:13 TM).

Clearly, the Shunmmite woman was not looking to move. She basically said, "I'm believing God to show up in *this* house and in *this* season. My husband and I have locked arms in partnership, and we're not giving up until God moves!"

Her response stirred Elisha's spirit even more. He could not rest until something was done to bless this woman.

> So he said, "What then is to be done for her?" And Gehazi answered, "Actually, she has no son, and her husband is old."
>
> So he said, "Call her." When he had called her, she stood in the doorway. Then he said, "About this time next year you shall embrace a son." And she said, "No, my lord. Man of God, do not lie to your maidservant!"
>
> But the woman conceived, and bore a son when the appointed time had come, of which Elisha had told her (2 Kings 4:14-17).

When Elisha's servant had called her, "she stood in the doorway." This wasn't just any doorway. It wasn't a doorway to the closet or the kitchen or the bathroom. It was the doorway to the upper room where Elisha stayed. It was the doorway built on the perception of what God was doing. It was the doorway built through the partnership of the Shunammite woman and her husband. It was a doorway that did not exist in the previous season. It was the doorway to a new dimension of God's presence.

The minute she stepped into the doorway, God spoke His word through Elisha: "About this time next year you shall embrace a son" (v. 16).

Elisha was saying, "Everything is about to change. This house is about to be turned upside-down! This house is about to receive new life. Before now, this house had no future. But a child is on the way, and your legacy is going to continue for another generation. Get ready!"

Staggering emotionally under the weight of the words that just entered her ears, the Shunammite woman said, in essence, "That's too good to be true. My husband and I are too old. We're beyond the season of childbearing. When I look at my husband and when I look in the mirror, I'm reminded of our limitations and the impossibility. Please, don't play games and speak such fantasies."

But the natural circumstances and physical limitations did not matter. They were no match for power of God. He had spoken and the impossible became possible! "The woman conceived, and bore a son when the appointed time had come, of which Elisha had told her" (v. 17).

How did she conceive? Through *continued partnership* with her husband and the blessing of God on their union. Remember, where there is unity, God commands His blessing.

PRAY FOR PURPOSEFUL PARTNERSHIPS.

As you stay *vertically* connected in a healthy relationship with God, you're in position to make a *horizontal* impact in the lives of others. Living in partnership with Him gives you power with people. Luke 2:52 says, "Jesus increased in wisdom and stature, and in favor with *God* and *men*." Jesus' favor was first with God and then with people. When you're properly connected with Heaven, it gives you power on earth.

Friend, you are stronger today because of the people God has placed around you—those who worship with you, serve with you, and lead you. Be thankful for the people He has placed in your life. Remember, anything is possible through the power of partnership. When the gifts in people come together at the right place in the right time, miracles happen. Together we are stronger. Together we are better!

I want to pray as we close this chapter:

> Father, I believe You're doing something in our lives right now! It's something we can only do as we stay vertically connected to You and horizontally connected with the people You've placed around us. I ask You to create a deeper desire in us to be in Your presence. Reveal and remove any negative influence trying to delay and derail

us from our purpose. Put the right people in our lives. Create divine partnerships with those who will help advance Your kingdom and fulfill our purpose. I declare that Your people are standing in a doorway to a new dimension of Your presence and have an appointment with destiny. I ask and declare these things in Jesus' name. Amen.

DISCOVERING YOUR DOORWAY

In light of what you've just read about the *power of partnership*, reflect on and respond to these personalized thoughts and questions.

• What is my greatest takeaway from this chapter? What is most important to me in this moment that I want to remember?

____

____

____

____

• I believe the **action steps** God is prompting me to take are:

____

____

____

____

• **Take time to pray.** "Lord, thank You for what You've shown me in this chapter. Please continue revealing to me the supernatural strength of partnership.

If there are any people in my life who are *wrong* for me, show me. If there are people around me You want me to partner with, reveal them. I'm trusting in You."

Now *listen* and *write* what He reveals.

NOTES

"You will be amazed at the progress you make if you'll simply be willing to start doing whatever God is leading you to do. It may not be lifting weights, but I am sure He is dealing with you about something because God is always urging us upward. Doing the difficult things God asks is what helps us build spiritual muscle."

—**Joyce Meyer**

Never Give Up!

5

IT'S TIME TO STRETCH

Have you ever found yourself between a rock and a hard place? Difficulty surrounds you on all sides, and there appears to be no way out. All of us go through times like these. If you're in one now, know that there's nothing wrong with you. In fact, there's probably something *right* with you, and God is just about ready to do something extraordinary right before your eyes.

Such was the case with the woman from Shunem. As we have seen, she and her husband were in a tough place. They had just come out of a famine in the land of Israel—a lack of both physical food and spiritual nourishment. They were aging and childless, and things looked bleak.

Then something changed. A man named Elisha came to Shunem. He was a mighty man of God—a powerful prophet anointed by the Holy Spirit. Suddenly, the Shunammite woman had a glimmer of hope. She perceived Elisha was a holy man filled with the supernatural power of God, and she was hungry for God's presence. To get him to stop by, she began preparing and providing delicious meals.

More! she thought. *There has to be more. There's just something about Elisha and the anointing of God on his life. I'm not content with occasional visits. I want him to stay with us.* To make this happen, it required partnership between the Shunammite woman and her husband. She said to him, "Please, let us make a small upper room on the wall; and let us put a bed for him there, and a table and a chair and a lampstand; so it will be, whenever he comes to us, he can turn in there" (2 Kings 4:10).

To expand their home required a great deal of *stretching*—including the stretching of their vision, their finances, and their faith. But their efforts paid off: "And it happened one day that he [Elisha] came there, and he turned in to the upper room and lay down there" (v. 11). Little did they know the full impact their willingness to stretch would produce. Supernatural blessings were about to be released. The doorway they built to the upper room became a gateway to their appointed breakthrough already on God's calendar. "About this time next year you shall embrace a son," Elisha said. "Sure enough, the woman soon became pregnant. And at that time the following year she had a son, just as Elisha had said" (v. 17 NLT).

What is God about to do in your life? Are you ready? It's time to stretch!

MOSES EXPERIENCED A TIME OF STRETCHING.

Moses and the children of Israel had been miraculously delivered from slavery in Egypt. Through a series of never-before-seen signs and wonders, God demonstrated His matchless might against the tyrant Pharaoh. God had brought His people out of bondage to freely worship Him in a new land. But just days after their departure, Moses and the Israelites found themselves between a rock and a hard place.

Once again, Pharaoh's heart was hardened against God. With haste, he rallied his choice chariots and armed warriors and took off in hot pursuit of the Israelites. Bent on returning them to the bondage from which they came, the mighty Egyptian army quickly caught up with and cornered the Israelites between the mountains on one side and the Red Sea on the other.

Take note: Israel's past wanted them back. Their enemies were hunting them down like dogs to keep them from their destiny. Please know that when your past wants you back that badly, there is great purpose in your future. There is great destiny in your tomorrow when your yesterday keeps trying to pull you back. Realize that what's before you is so much better than what is behind you. God's power is infinitely stronger, and He'll get you to where He's called you to be—just as He did for the Israelites.

Your future is not in your past. It's not in your last mistake, and it's not in your last choice that was not pleasing to God. You are human just like everyone else. You don't always make choices that are in alignment with the will or the Word of God. But you don't have to live there. Failure is not your permanent address. God's "goodness and mercy" is where you live (Psalm 23:6). If you mess up, fess up. Simply and sincerely ask God for His forgiveness and His grace, and move on (see 1 John 1:9).

There the Israelites were—trapped between their enemies, the mountainous rocks, and the Red Sea. It looked like they had nowhere to turn. Then God spoke to Moses and told him to do three things: stand up, speak out, and stretch.

STAND UP.

Clearly, Moses was in a tough place. With Pharaoh and his henchmen breathing down the necks of the Israelites and obstacles on every side, great fear infiltrated the camp. Immediately, the people began to murmur and complain. "Then they said to Moses, 'Because there were no graves in Egypt, have you taken us away to die in the wilderness? Why have you so dealt with us, to bring us up out of Egypt? . . . For it would have been better for us to serve the Egyptians than that we should die in the wilderness'" (Exodus 14:11-12).

When the heat was on, the children of Israel looked back at their previous place of captivity and saw it as a place of comfort. Their walk through the wilderness on the way to the Promised Land was full of great difficulty, and they longed for the comfort of what they were familiar with back in Egypt. We tend to react the same way. But the idea that our former bondage is somehow better than the freedom that awaits us is a lie. The freedom God has called us to live in is well worth walking through any uncomfortable places. Going back to what used to be is not an option for God's children. We've got to *stand up* and *move forward* into the freedom He's promised.

That's what God told Moses to do. "Then the Lord said to Moses, 'Quit praying and get the people moving! Forward, march!'" (Exodus 14:15 TLB) In other words, "Stand up, Moses! Rise above your current situation. Don't listen to the murmuring and complaining of the people. Don't look at your enemies who are chomping at the bit to bring you down. Stand up and move forward!"

The prophet Isaiah said it this way: "Arise [from the depression and prostration in which circumstances have kept you—rise to a new life]! Shine (be radiant with the glory of the Lord), for your light has come, and the glory of the Lord has risen upon you!" (Isaiah 60:1 AMPC).

I believe this is a word from God for you. Arise! Stand up! Don't let depressing circumstances and situations keep you down another day. Get up and begin walking and living in the abundant, radiant life Christ has provided.

SPEAK OUT.

God also told Moses to *speak out.* If you read Moses' backstory, you'll discover he had a problem speaking. At times he stuttered, stammered, and stumbled all over himself to find the right words to say.

God will always challenge your areas of weakness as you're walking through the wilderness. He will ask you to do things you feel totally unable to do so you will depend totally on Him. This way He gets *all* the glory for the victory in your life. Remember His promise: "My strength and power are made perfect (fulfilled and completed) and show themselves most effective in [your] weakness" (2 Corinthians 12:9 AMPC).

Although Moses had struggled with speaking, he chose to stand up and speak God's message of hope to the children of Israel: "Do not be afraid. Stand still, and see the salvation of the Lord, which He will accomplish for you today. For the Egyptians whom you see today, you shall see again no more forever. The Lord will fight for you, and you shall hold your peace" (Exodus 14:13-14).

Whatever you're going through, whatever weaknesses have raised their ugly heads, push past your fears and flaws and trust God. "Humble yourselves in the sight of the Lord, and He will lift you up" (James 4:10).

STRETCH OUT.

Next, God instructed Moses to walk to the edge of the Red Sea and *stretch*. The Bible says, "Then Moses *stretched out* his hand over the sea; and the Lord caused the sea to go back by a strong east wind all that night, and made the sea into dry land, and the waters were divided. So the children of Israel went into the midst of the sea on the dry ground, and the waters were a wall to them on their right hand and on their left" (Exodus 14:21-22).

If you're willing to stretch, God will take you places you've never been before. He will make a way where there seems to be no way—even create an impossible path of deliverance through your sea of problems. As Moses came to the edge of everything he knew and everything he could see and *stretched*, God's power showed up! Scripture says, "The Lord caused the sea to go back by a strong east wind all that night." In your midnight hour, God will go to work on your behalf if you're willing to stretch and do what He's telling you to do.

After the sea had parted and the children of Israel crossed on dry ground, *more stretching* was required.

> The Lord said to Moses, "Stretch out your hand over the sea, that the waters may come back upon the Egyptians, on their chariots, and on their horsemen." And Moses stretched out his hand over the sea; and when the morning appeared, the sea returned to its full depth, while the Egyptians

> were fleeing into it. So the Lord overthrew the Egyptians in the midst of the sea. Then the waters returned and covered the chariots, the horsemen, and all the army of Pharaoh that came into the sea after them. Not so much as one of them remained (vv. 26-28).

The stretching God required of Moses took time, energy, and effort. I'm sure he became weary in the process. Even so, he was obedient and did not give up. And because he was willing to stretch, God not only opened a doorway to a new season; He also destroyed Israel's archenemies in the process. With their own eyes, they watched as the world's mightiest army was swallowed by the sea and then washed up on the shore.

However God is asking you to stretch, He will equip and enable you to do it. The enemy would want you to believe what God is asking you to do is just too hard. But that's a lie. God's Word declares: "What I am commanding you today is not too difficult for you or beyond your reach. . . . No, the word is very near you; it is in your mouth and in your heart so you may obey it" (Deuteronomy 30:11, 14 NIV1984).

If you will be obedient to *stand up*, *speak out*, and *stretch*, God will honor your faith. He will move into your life and into your situation, and things will begin to change. It's time to stretch!

A WOMAN'S STRETCH FAITH DOWN IN 'BAMA

Many years ago when I had just started out in ministry, I was preaching at a large church in Birmingham,

Alabama; and it was lively, Sprit-filled church. When I say lively, I mean it was off-the-chain Pentecostal. The meetings, which were originally scheduled for one weekend, turned into a spontaneous five-week revival. The place was packed every night. The Spirit of God moved mightily. It was truly amazing to see and be part of that revival.

On one particular night, I remember teaching about allowing God to use us and stretch us. At the end of the service, we opened the altar for prayer, and a lady I had never met came down to the front. She was quiet, petite, and reserved. I prayed for her like I had prayed for many others that evening. Essentially the prayer was, "Lord, if You can use anything, use us to bring You glory." After I prayed with her, nothing visible happened. She didn't fall down or run around the building or scream exuberantly. She just quietly returned to her seat.

The next day, she went to work and began telling everyone about the services at the church and what God was doing. At that time, I was back at the hotel where I was staying when suddenly the phone rang, and it was this woman. She had called the church where I was speaking, and they gave her the name and number of my hotel.

"Pastor Tony," she said softly, "you probably don't remember me, but I was at the altar last night. Usually, I'm really shy and quiet, and to call you like this is totally out of my nature. But after you prayed with me last night, and I came to work and began telling everybody about what God is doing in the meetings. Normally, I keep to myself, but I just couldn't keep quiet about how God is touching people at our church."

A smile came to my face. Although it was unusual and a bit startling to get a phone call from a church member where I was ministering, I was encouraged that God was stretching this woman to be a witness for Him. She continued.

"While I was on my break this morning, a lady came to talk to me about the revival. She said, 'We go to a Catholic church, but I was thinking about coming to your church. My son has been very sick. He has some type of bacteria and illness in his stomach, and the doctors can't figure out what it is. He hasn't eaten solid food for almost a month, and he has lost 80 pounds. The really sad thing is my son is supposed to attend college next year and play football on a scholarship. But because of this sickness and the weight loss, he's about to lose his scholarship, and he's just a wreck. His whole world is caving in, and he's become very depressed.'

"Pastor Tony," the woman continued, "I don't know why, but I just encouraged her to come to church tonight and bring her son and that if she did, the Lord would heal him."

At that moment, I was on the other end of the phone thinking, *Oh, Lord! If he comes tonight, You better heal him!* Although I had some faith, I also had some doubt, and I could feel the pressure mounting.

"Wow! That's great!" I told her. "Yeah, you go ahead and bring them to church."

Immediately, my mind was off to the races. *They're Catholic*, I thought. *Okay, that means we need to break them into the Pentecostal scene gently. Lord, let's maybe have a slower service tonight. You know, one that's toned down, calmer.*

Well, the service that night was anything but calm. In fact, from the very beginning it was like wildfire. Things were so out of the ordinary, I didn't even get to preach. As the praise and worship went up, pandemonium came down. The altars filled up quickly, and people were boldly and exuberantly expressing the power of the Holy Spirit throughout the building.

If this Catholic woman and her son are here, I thought, *they probably think we're crazy right about now.*

Then about halfway through the prayer time, I distinctly remember seeing a tall young man from the middle section stand and begin making his way down to the front. As he stepped into the aisle and began walking forward with his mother, I could see he looked like skin and bones. The minute I saw them, I knew who they were.

I met him near the stage and introduced myself.

"Hi, I'm Eric," he said softly.

"Can I pray with you, Eric?" I asked.

"Yeah," he responded.

"Do you believe God can heal you tonight?" I questioned. And with the nod of his head, he answered yes.

At that point, he began to look around a bit. He probably didn't understand everything that was going on, but he did sense God's presence. So, I laid my hands on him and began to pray, and he instantly gained 80 pounds!

No, that's not what happened. That would have been amazingly cool if it had, but it didn't. Actually, Eric didn't fall to the ground, scream loudly like some of the other people had done that night, nor exhibit much emotion. Instead, he stood there and calmly shed a few tears.

I looked at him and said, "Eric, I'm believing God is going to heal you, and you're going to be playing football this next year, and you'll even start as a freshman!"

He laughed and went back to his seat.

I didn't think much more about it until the next day when I received another phone call at my hotel room.

"Hello, Pastor Tony?" the voice said. "I'm Eric's mom. You prayed for him last night at the service."

"Yes," I said. "I remember him. What can I do for you?'

"I hope I'm not bothering you," she said, "but I really wanted to call you and give you a testimony about

Eric. He had not eaten solid food for about a month. But this morning he got up and said, 'Mom, I'm so hungry for pancakes. I'm just craving pancakes.' So I made him the biggest batch of pancakes I've ever made, and Eric ate every one of them!"

It wasn't long before Eric gained all of his weight back and went on to play college football for four years. He even started as a freshman!

The point of my story is simple: God will use anyone who allows Him to stretch them. That shy woman who sat on the back row and came forward for prayer that night in Birmingham allowed God to stretch her faith. She said, "Lord, if You can use anything, I believe You can use me." It was not in her nature to walk around and tell others about God and what He was doing in her church, but she went to the edge of everything she knew and stretched. As a result of her willingness to stretch, other people's lives were powerfully impacted! Eric and his mom were forever changed because of her obedience and faith.

THE SHUNAMMITE WOMAN WAS WILLING TO STRETCH.

Throughout the Word of God, He has required His people to be willing to stretch in order to enlarge their lives and lead them into greater places. The Shunammite woman perceived God was moving through the prophet Elisha, and she wanted to get in on what God was about to do. In faith, she reached out to her husband and asked him to partner with her, and he agreed. I believe what she said to him may have sounded something like this:

> We've just come through a lean season, and we've walked through some tough battles. But I perceive this man Elisha who passes by regularly is a holy man. The powerful presence of God is with him. I know it will be a stretch for us, but if we work together and use what God has given us, I believe He is going to do something amazing in the days ahead.
>
> We've got this little area up here on the top of our house, and I can imagine a little room being built up there. I can see it furnished with a bed, a table, a chair, and a lampstand. If we can stretch a little bit and enlarge our home, I believe God will move into it. It will expand our house to new heights and lift our lives to a new level.
>
> So let's stretch and make more room for God's presence to dwell in our home, in our circumstances, and in our situations. I believe if God shows up, everything else will begin to work out. Our finances will come into alignment. Our marriage will come into alignment. And all the other things we're struggling with will come into alignment with what God is doing. In His presence is freedom. In His presence is victory. In His presence is fullness of joy.

WHAT IS GOD CALLING YOU TO DO RIGHT NOW?

How is He asking you to stretch? What are you on the edge of that you have never done before? It's time to stretch! Pray and make this declaration to God:

> Lord, I believe this next season is going to be greater than all the other seasons before it. Even though many things that could go wrong have gone wrong, I'm believing my next season is a blessed season. It's a season of breakthrough! It's a season of turnaround! It's a season of overcoming faith, and I'm going to soar to new heights by Your grace.

Friend, the Lord wants to take those small places in your life and stretch them into large places. He will meet you in every place you obediently choose to stretch. If you will stretch, He will take you to places you never thought you could go. If you will stretch, the goodness of the Lord will be there to meet you. If you will stretch, you will be blessed and experience God's best.

It's time to stretch.

DISCOVERING YOUR DOORWAY

In light of what you just read, "It's Time to Stretch," reflect on and respond to these personalized thoughts and questions.

• What is my **greatest takeaway** from this chapter? What is most important to me in this moment that I want to remember?

____

____

____

____

• I believe the **action steps** God is prompting me to take are:

____
____
____
____

• Take time to **pray**: "Lord, where are You asking me to stretch in my life right now? What are You trying to teach me and build in me?"

Listen and *write* what He reveals. Ask Him to help you trust Him and praise Him, regardless of what you see or how you feel.

____
____
____
____

NOTES

"What is that in your hand?

That is the question the Lord asked of Moses. It's the same question He asks of us. . . . You may be tempted to think, 'I can't make much of a difference anyway.' And you can't as long as you hang on to what you have. But if you put the two fish you have in your hands into God's hands, God can feed five thousand with it."

—Mark Batterson

All In

6

USE WHAT'S IN YOUR HAND

In the last chapter, we discovered experiencing the fullness of what God has for us often requires a time of *stretching*—going to the edge of everything we know and everything we can see and obediently stepping out to do what God is asking us to do. We see this scenario play out in the lives of God's people all throughout His Word, including the woman from Shunem.

With the stretching, God also often requires us to take and use what He's given us in order to advance His kingdom and bring Him glory. While He will never ask us for something we don't have, He will ask us to surrender to Him what we do have. Our time, our talent, our treasure, and our testimony are all resources in our hands that God wants us to manage and invest as He directs.

For the Shunammite woman and her husband, God had prepared a great destiny. To get them to and through the doorway of blessing, He required them to stretch their faith. Specifically, He asked them to invest their time, their talent, and their treasure to expand their home and make room for His presence by making room for Elisha the prophet. Their obedience revolutionized their world. It ushered them into a season of multiplication and breakthrough beyond their wildest hopes and dreams. The impossible became possible. In their old age, they miraculously conceived and gave birth to a son, and it came about because they used what God had placed in their hands.

GOD WORKED WONDERS FOR A WIDOW AND HER TWO SONS.

In the same chapter where the Shunammite's story is found, there's another amazing account demonstrating the power of using what's in your hand. A widow of one of the prophets was deeply in debt and about to lose her greatest possession—her two sons. Her story begins in Second Kings 4:1:

> A certain woman of the wives of the sons of the prophets cried out to Elisha, saying, "Your servant my husband is dead, and you know that your servant feared the Lord. And the creditor is coming to take my two sons to be his slaves."

Like the Shunammite woman, this widow lived during a time of famine in Israel. Her husband had died, and the creditor was coming to take her two sons to work off her and her husband's debt as his slaves. Her boys were not just her present joy—they were her future. By law they were required to work and provide for their mother. With them about to be seized from the family, things looked terribly bleak.

Think about it. As a result of the widow's past, her present was a mess, and the enemy was trying to destroy her future. The same thing often happens in our lives. We find ourselves enslaved in the present because of what happened in our past—including things that were out of our control. How did God respond to the widow's cry of desperation? "So Elisha said to her, 'What shall I do for you? Tell me, what do you have in the house?'" (2 Kings 4:2a).

In other words, Elisha said, "You've told me about what you *don't* have and about the creditor who is on his way to enslave your sons. Now tell me about what you *do* have. What has God placed in your hands and given you to steward?" She said, "Your maidservant has nothing in the house but a jar of oil" (v. 2b).

To this, Elisha, who represented the voice of God, replied:

> "Go, borrow vessels from everywhere, from all your neighbors—empty vessels; do not gather just a few. And when you have come in, you shall shut the door behind you and your sons; then pour it into all those vessels, and set aside the full ones" (vv. 3-4).

Elisha basically told her, "Take what's in your hand and use it. Utilize what God has given you, and He will multiply your resources. Yes, it will require faith, and yes, you're going to have to be willing to stretch. But if you will trust God, ask your neighbors for as many empty vessels as they're willing to loan you, and begin pouring out what God has entrusted to you. He will miraculously bless your obedience." This was the word of the Lord to the widow.

Clearly, God's word through Elisha made no sense in the natural. In fact, He challenged the widow to stretch her faith in the very area the enemy was trying to destroy her. God will often do the same thing in your life. He will call you to step up and step out. He will require you to stretch so your faith overrides your doubt and everything else you see and hear that's trying to sabotage and steal your future.

The widow did just that. She and her sons went out and borrowed vessels from everyone everywhere. They then took every container they had gathered and returned to their house. What happened next was nothing short of a miracle.

> She went from him and shut the door behind her and her sons, who brought the vessels to her; and she poured it out. Now it came to pass, when the vessels were full, that she said to her son, "Bring me another vessel." And he said to her, "There is not another vessel." So the oil ceased (vv. 5-6).

Are you seeing this? The enemy was about to steal, kill, and destroy this widow and her sons. Their hope for the present and future was on the brink of extinction. She cried out to God for help, and He answered her through His servant Elisha. His instructions required her to stretch her faith and use the resource within her hand. She obeyed, and God showed up!

Any time you stretch out in faith and surrender to God what He is asking of you, the Holy Spirit will begin to move. For the widow and her sons, the oil—which is a symbol of the Holy Spirit—began to multiply and fill every vessel. As long as they were stretching their faith, trusting God to multiply the resources He had given them, the oil continued to flow. The moment that all the vessels were full, the oil stopped flowing.

> Then she came and told the man of God. And he said, "Go, sell the oil and pay your debt; and you and your sons live on the rest" (v. 7).

Elisha told the widow, "Use what's in your hand. Take all the containers of oil God has miraculously multiplied through your obedience and sell them. The small amount you initially held in your hand couldn't do a thing for you. But now that you have surrendered it to the Lord, He has produced a mighty surplus—not only to pay off all your debt, but also for you and your sons to begin living your life to the full!"

What has God placed in *your* hands? What is He asking *you* to stretch out in faith and use? God doesn't want to bring you to the point of poverty or even to the brink of barely getting by. He wants to bring you to the place of overcoming overflow! What miracle awaits *you* on the other side of your obedience? Why not step out and find out?

GOD WANTS YOU TO BE A GOOD STEWARD OF WHAT HE'S GIVEN YOU.

In every area of your life in which God has given you authority, He has called you to steward well. What you have been given, you have authority over and responsibility to manage wisely. Personally, God has called me to steward my family, my finances, and my ministry with excellence. He also requires me to wisely oversee my health, my thoughts, and my words.

The truth is, you and I have no authority over what we don't possess. That is, we cannot steward or manage what is not ours. As close as I am to my pastor friends, I cannot steward their lives. I can encourage them, pray for them, and even offer them godly wisdom for the decisions they need to make. But ultimately, only they can steward what God has given them—only they can stretch out in faith and obediently use what's in their hands to experience God's blessings.

The Shunammite woman didn't say to her husband, "Let's build an upper room on our neighbor's house," or, "Let's make a room for Elisha in my parents' garage." She said, "Let's make a room on the wall of *our* house. Let's take some of *our* resources and furnish it with a bed, a table, a chair, and a lampstand." The Shunammite woman and her husband stretched out in faith and used what was in their hand, and God blessed it.

While there are countless things we are each called to steward, there are four primary areas I want to take a moment to focus on. They are our *time*, our *talent*, our *treasure* and our *testimony*. Let's briefly take a look at each of these.

STEWARD YOUR TIME.

Everyone has been given the same amount of *time* each day. You don't have more than your neighbors, and they don't have more than you. Contrary to what some may think, God doesn't give some people more hours in the day because they are "more important" or have a lot to do. As a pastor, I get the same amount of time as everyone else—twenty-four hours. And I must learn to steward them wisely.

God tells us in Ephesians 5:15-16, "See then that you walk circumspectly, not as fools but as wise, *redeeming the time*, because the days are evil." Are you a good steward of your time? Are you making the most out of the hours you are given each day to know and fulfill God's plan and purpose for your life? Time is a resource He has placed in your hand, and He wants you to steward it wisely.

STEWARD YOUR TALENT.

Each of us has also been given *talent* from God to do specific things well. Talent comes in the form of natural and supernatural abilities, and in both cases they are given to us to be a blessing to others. The Bible says, "Each person is given something to do that shows who God is: Everyone get in on it, everyone benefits" (1 Corinthians 12:7 TM).

God wants you to be a good steward of your talent. He wants you to use your gifts to show others who He is and advance His kingdom. Sadly, there are a number of believers who have allowed their talents to become dormant. Some have even buried them out of fear. Whatever the case may be, they're not using the special gifting and ability God has placed in their hands. If this describes you, it's time to make some changes.

Please realize, those who don't *use* their talents will *lose* their talents. We see this demonstrated in the Word of God (see Matthew 25:14-30; Luke 19:12-26). On the flip side, those who use their talents wisely will receive even more. Therefore, since "God has given each of you some special abilities; be sure to use them to help each other, passing on to others God's many kinds of blessings" (1 Peter 4:10 TLB). God himself will sharpen your gifts and make them grow with each use!

STEWARD YOUR TREASURE.

In addition to your time and talent, God also wants you to be a good steward of your *treasure*. For some, this is the most difficult thing of all to manage. Jesus said, "For where your treasure is, there your heart will be also" (Matthew 6:21). In other words, what you love you will invest in financially.

I have discovered that people don't have money issues in their lives—they have *heart* issues. That is, there are things in their heart that cause them to be greedy instead of generous. They have fears and false perceptions about finances that cause them to close their hand instead of open it to help meet the needs of others.

Think about it. When it comes to your treasure, which word would better describe you: a *conduit* or a *reservoir*? One who is a reservoir is *always receiving* and never giving. In Bible times, the people living in the towns of Chorazin and Bethsaida were reservoirs. They had experienced many mighty works at the hands of Jesus, yet there was no repentance for their sin. All they did was receive—they never gave anything back. As a result, Jesus said they would be judged more harshly than the towns of Tyre and Sidon on Judgment Day (see Matthew 11:21-22).

God does not bless stingy people. He himself is a giver, and He blesses those who follow His example. The Bible says, "For God so loved the world that He *gave* his only begotten Son . . ." (John 3:16). God gave His very best and held nothing back so we might have our relationship with Him restored and spend eternity with Him in Heaven. If all you are is a reservoir, you're cutting yourself off from God's blessings. He instead wants you to be a conduit through which He can flow. The more He can get *through* you, the more He will get *to* you.

Interestingly, the area of giving is the only area in which God offers the challenge to "test" Him. "'Test me in this,' says the Lord Almighty, 'and see if I will not throw open the floodgates of heaven and pour out so much blessing that you will not have room enough to store it'" (Malachi 3:10 NIV 1984). Being a good steward of your treasure causes the floodgates, or windows, of Heaven to open! And when the windows of Heaven open, the supernatural invades the natural. God's "super" gets on your "natural," and what you couldn't do on your own begins to happen.

There are things you desire to see in your life that will only happen as you obediently begin to release your treasure. I encourage you to allow God to begin working on this area of your heart. Let Him free you from any fears and misconceptions about finances. Cooperate with Him and ask Him to cultivate a heart of generosity in you—not just in giving to the church, but also in giving to others.

God promises us, "Give, and it will be given to you: good measure, pressed down, shaken together, and running over will be put into your bosom. For with the same measure that you use, it will be measured back to you" (Luke 6:38). Whatever we give to others—a kind attitude, undivided attention, encouraging words, material possessions, money, whatever—is a seed that will reap a harvest.

STEWARD YOUR TESTIMONY.

You and I are also called to be good stewards of our *testimony*. This does not mean you need to walk around at work waving a big Bible or have an intercessory prayer meeting during your lunch break. It simply means you live your life in such a way that people can clearly see you're different. It also means that when someone asks you why you're different, you have an answer to give them.

The Bible says, "If anybody asks why you believe as you do, be ready to tell him, and do it in a gentle and respectful way" (1 Peter 3:15 TLB). You should be amazed at the power your testimony packs. Something as simple as, "If it had not been for Jesus coming into my life, I don't know where I'd be right now," can be life-changing for someone to hear.

How you steward your time, talent, and treasure are all a part of stewarding your testimony. So steward your testimony well! Live your life as a representative of God's kingdom and His Word everywhere you go. Not just on Sunday, but on Monday, Tuesday, Wednesday, Thursday, Friday, and Saturday. When you live like Jesus during the week, people will want to come to church with you on the weekend. *Share your story!*

EXPECT TO REAP A HARVEST ON EVERYTHING YOU INVEST.

When you take what's in your hand and obediently put it to use, you are making an investment that will always pay off. Investing in the kingdom of God—in His plan for your life and the lives of others—is like planting good seed in fertile soil. It will *always* produce a good harvest.

Galatians 6:7 says, "Do not be deceived, God is not mocked; for whatever a man sows, that he will also reap." Many believers look at this promise only from a negative point of view. However, there's also a very positive side. That is, when you generously sow your time, talent, and treasure into the cause of Christ in any way, you will reap a harvest of blessings. Likewise, when you invest your effort, energy, and existence into helping others, you're setting in motion God's purpose and plan, which is a powerful thing.

In Jeremiah 29:11, God says, "For I know the plans I have for you, . . . plans to prosper you and not to harm you, plans to give you hope and a future" (NIV1984). The plan of God is always beyond you—it is future-focused and beyond figuring out. Yet, at the same time, it is always connected to your present. His plan always promotes and blesses you—it never harms you. As you invest in His plan, you are actually building your future.

It may be that you're in a season of planting right now, and you may have been in it for a very long time.

You've been sowing seeds in the form of good deeds, worship, praise, and prayers. You've been unselfishly giving of your time, talent, and treasure to see others come to Christ and be changed into His image. Rest assured, God sees every sacrifice you've made and heard every prayer you've prayed. Your investment is not in vain!

David sowed kindness, goodness, and mercy for many years before he became king. Noah labored long and hard for decades, building a boat when there was no water to make it float. Abraham invested years of trust and obedience into his relationship with God. He even surrendered his son and was willing to sacrifice him in worship to the Lord, not knowing how God's promise would come to pass in his life. None of them gave up, and God proved Himself faithful to each of them.

Some of the greatest times of ministry for my wife, Kaci, and me were not when we were in a season of abundance but in a season of battle. The enemy had come in and was pressing hard against us. But we made up our minds to press through his attacks and overcome his delays. We decided to rise above all the noise and continue to invest in what God was doing, and we were never disappointed with the outcome.

WHAT IS IT FOR YOU?

Friend, you may be on the edge of the biggest breakthrough you have ever experienced. Right now, God is saying, "I just need you to stretch out in faith.

I need you to take what I've placed in your hand and allow Me to do something with it."

For Moses, it was his staff.

For Sampson, it was his strength . . . and a donkey's jawbone.

For Hannah, it was her son Samuel.

For Esther, it was her Jewish identity.

For Mary, it was her reputation.

For the little boy in the crowd, it was his lunch of five loaves and two fish.

What is it for you? What has God placed in your hand that He's asking you to use *right now*?

If you'll use it, He will multiply it—beyond what you can do yourself, beyond anything you can imagine. He wants to take you, your family, your business, and your ministry and expand it so greatly that when you look back to where you are now, you'll know that what happened could've only been by His hand and power on your life!

God is faithful! He will keep His Word. What you sow, you will reap. As you give, it will be given back to you. This is not just a cute Christian cliché; it is an unchanging, unbreakable spiritual law. So, "Let us not grow weary while doing good, for in due season we shall reap if we do not lose heart" (Galatians 6:9).

Use what's in your hand.

DISCOVERING YOUR DOORWAY

In light of what you just read in this chapter, "Use What's in Your Hand," reflect on and respond to these personalized thoughts and questions.

• What is my **greatest takeaway** from this chapter? What is most important to me in this moment that I want to remember?

____

____

____

• I believe the **action steps** God is prompting me to take are:

____

____

____

____

• Take time to **pray**: "Lord, what have You placed in my hand that You want me to put to use right now? Please show me and give me the strength to stretch out in faith and do what You're asking me to do."

Listen and *write* what He reveals. Ask Him to help you trust Him and praise Him, regardless of what you see or how you feel.

____

____

____

____

"The opportunity of a lifetime must be seized within the lifetime of the opportunity."

—Leonard Ravenhill

7

SEIZE THE MOMENT

The threshold of the doorway is a strategic place. It's the point of exit from one season and an entry point into the next. It's what I call the place of "to." When God is moving us, He moves us from season to season, from glory to glory. It's those two little letters—the *T* and the *O*—in the journey that so often get overlooked. Without them, the journey of our yesterday and the promise of our tomorrow do not connect.

For the Shunamite woman, the threshold *to* her new season was the doorway of the room she and her husband had built for Elisha the prophet. The Bible says:

> So he [Elisha] said, "Call her." When he had called her, she stood in the doorway. Then he said, "About this time next year you shall embrace a son" (2 Kings 4:15-16).

The old season for the Shunammite woman and her husband was one of barrenness. The new season they were entering would be one of newness of life and great joy. When we read the conversation that took place between Elisha and the Shunammite, we see a threshold is where we're no longer where we used to be, but we're still not where we're going. It is the place where our faith is stretched and challenged—a place of transition where we battle doubts and fears, and God is aligning us for the next season.

Sometimes the transition into the new season is quick, and other times it's a time of waiting that seems to never end. Think about David. The threshold of his new season was the moment Samuel anointed him to be the next king of Israel (see 1 Samuel 16:12-13). However, his transition out of the old season of shepherding into the new season of kingship took nearly fifteen years of preparation. As David waited for God to move him, he continued to watch sheep, carry lunch to his brothers, and learn the art of writing songs and worshiping. In addition to killing a giant and building his faith, David was given a front-row seat to watch King Saul and learn what to do and what not to do.

Exactly how long our time of transition—and preparation—will be is unknown and is not to be our focus. What's most important is recognizing and seizing the moments God places before us. Many times in life and in our journey of faith, we are longing to get into the next season. Instead, we need to keep our spiritual eyes open for the God-moments He brings our way. I call it "the power of now." That unexpected connection, that random encounter, that door which opens suddenly—these divine moments are the game-changers of life. They not only reveal and release us into our next season but also unlock the door to seasons to come.

GOD GIVES *NOW* MOMENTS.

A few years ago I experienced a divine "now" moment that changed the trajectory of our lives and our church forever. Honestly, we were so busy battling to get from one season to the next that the moment could have very easily been missed. I was on a mission trip in the mountains of Nicaragua—preaching, teaching, and encouraging the local pastors. I'll never forget one particular stop we made in a small, isolated village. The bishop who had planned our trip and our translator were checking on one of the pastors they knew.

The moment I walked up and was introduced to this man, I felt the Holy Spirit say to me, "Tell this pastor that you will build him a church." Now, I had never met this pastor before or been to this region. Likewise, I knew nothing about the church or even if they wanted a new building. Up until that time, the Holy Spirit had never challenged me to sow that type of seed. Yet I felt very strongly that God had spoken and instructed us to build them a church.

For the next few minutes, we sat and listened intently to the pastor as he shared through our translator the story of the church and his village. The people were hungry for God, and every week several hundred from the area would pack inside a small house for a worship service. After hearing him share his heart and being graciously served by him and his family, I asked, "Do you have any plans on building a church?"

A gentle smile washed over his face, and he quickly ran into the little house he was living in and came back out with a set of hand-drawn sketches of a new church building. He carefully laid them out in front of us, and we began to look them over together. Then he took our entire team to a vacant lot they had purchased with money they had raised. "We have been believing God for a new building," the pastor said.

Again, I heard the Holy Spirit say, "Tell him you will help him build a church."

So I asked, "How much will it cost to build this church?"

"About $25,000 U.S. dollars," he replied.

By most standards, that was very minimal to build a church. However, at that time in our ministry, $25,000 was like $250,000. We were a congregation of a few hundred people, and my wife and I had only been at citylife church a few years. Financially we were barely getting by. Our congregation had been around for eighty years, and our building was quite old and in need of repairs. I could not see us pulling together that kind of money. Yet, I somehow finally found enough faith and courage to open my mouth and say, "We're going to build you a church! We are going to give you the $25,000 you need to get it done."

Overwhelmed with joy, he ran into the house, called his family together, and excitedly shared the news. They all began to celebrate and cry tears of joy. I began to cry too, but it was because I knew we had no money. Still, I believed the Holy Spirit had spoken to me, and I had a sense of peace that He was going to help us fulfill our commitment.

FEAR ALWAYS FIGHTS US IN THE NOW MOMENTS.

After exchanging information and saying goodbye, I got back in the car to return to the hotel where we were staying. Immediately, the enemy began to bombard my mind with thoughts of fear and condemnation. The attack was so strong it was like Satan was sitting in the car right next to me.

You're crazy! he said. *Where in the world do you think you're going to get an extra $25,000 to build somebody else a church? You're just one week away from being broke yourself. You're going to disappoint this pastor and embarrass your church. You should have never made such a promise.*

I'll admit that on the surface, things didn't look good. With our own church in such disrepair and transition, we needed every dollar that came in to pay our overhead and fund our renovations. *What have I gotten us into?* I thought. *How are we going to raise the money to do this?* Feelings of defeat hung over me the entire ride back to the hotel.

Once we reached the city of Estelle where we were staying, my cell phone regained a signal and began to light up. I had received multiple voice messages while we were in the remote mountainous region. Some were from staff members and others were from numbers I didn't recognize. One message in particular piqued my interest, as it was from a professional football player from the Tampa Bay Buccaneers.

"Hey, Pastor Tony," the caller said. "I want to talk to you about your church building." No other details were given. I hit redial to return his call.

"I'd be happy to meet with you," I said, "I'll be home on Monday, and we can chat then." After arranging a time to meet, I hung up the phone and didn't think much more about it. Honestly, I thought he just wanted to use our building for a special event. But when Monday rolled around, he showed up with an entourage of thirteen people—people who had great resources. In fact, one of the families represented owned an NFL football team. Without delay, they made their wishes known.

EXPECT THE UNEXPECTED.

"Pastor, we want to talk to you about buying your church building," the person I had spoken to said.

Shocked by his request, I asked, "This church building? This forty-year-old church building? Why would you want to buy this?"

At that time, we were in the middle of an economic recession, and our church was in the middle of "the hood." No one was standing in line to buy a forty-year-old church building. Their request didn't make any sense.

"Well, Pastor," the man continued, "we have a charter school for inner-city, underprivileged kids that we want to expand. The city officials have granted us permission to do so, but we have to stay in this area. Your building is the only one that will work for us."

Instantly, I looked at them and boldly said, "For us to sell our building, it would take eight million dollars." I'm not sure why that number jumped out of my spirit. We had had several appraisals done, and on paper, our building and property was only worth two to three million—and that's if we could get a buyer. With that said, our meeting quickly ended and the visitors left. I went about my business and put the whole thing out of my mind.

A few days later, an attorney representing the charter school group called me. After he introduced himself, he said, "Pastor Stewart, all of the directors recently met, and they've decided to take it."

"Take what?" I asked.

"Your building," he replied. "They've agreed to your price of eight million dollars and are prepared to buy your building."

"Our building?" I answered in shock. "Well, I haven't even talked to my board or my wife about it yet, nor have I really prayed about it. You'll have to give me a few days."

Immediately, I knew in my heart it was a God moment—an unexpected moment when He rapidly moves in and invades our life with an unprecedented opportunity. I promptly met with my board of directors and shared what had happened. I asked them to join me and my wife, Kaci, in prayer. Unanimously, we felt God was involved in the offer we'd been given, and it was a Kingdom moment we couldn't pass up. The major hurdle would be finding a place to relocate.

THE OBSTACLES WE FACE ARE OPPORTUNITIES FOR GOD TO SHINE.

Then next day I was driving through the city of Tampa, and just after passing the stadium where the Buccaneers play, I drove through the intersection of Waters and Dale Mabry, which is the third busiest intersection in our city. As I did, there were workers taking down a sign for a large grocery store that had closed. After reading the "For Sale" sign and seeing it was 70,000 square feet, I sensed in my spirit that the building was for us. I quickly jotted down the phone number of the real-estate office handling the property and gave them a call.

"We want to buy the building you have for sale," I said confidently.

"Really?" the man chuckled. "Well, thanks for calling, Pastor, but this property is prime real estate in this city. There are presently twenty-three people standing in line to buy this building, and many of them are large national retail corporations. We appreciate your interest, but we're going to go with one of them most likely." I hung up the phone, and my faith was severely deflated.

When I got up the next morning, I could not get that old supermarket out of my mind. I truly believed we had walked into a now moment sent by God. Again, I felt a stirring inside to call the real-estate office. After several rings, someone finally answered, and I asked to speak with the same person I had talked to the day before.

"He's out sick," the receptionist replied.

"Then may I speak with his boss?" I asked. And with that I was promptly put on hold.

"I'm Josh, the supervisor of who you spoke to yesterday," the gentleman said. "How can I help you?" As polite as I could be, I began to tell the man our story, starting back at the mission trip in the mountains of Nicaragua. I told him how we pledged to build a church for the pastor there and how when we arrived back in the states, a group wanted to buy our building.

"Sir," I said respectfully, "We need to buy your building because we need a place to worship and re-establish our church." When I had finished telling our story, there was dead silence for what seemed like an eternity. Finally, he began to speak.

"Well, Pastor, I'm the vice president of this company, and I help the board come to a conclusion and make decisions in such cases as these. But I'm also the chairman of the mission board of my church in Atlanta. Our next company meeting is in California. When I get there, I'm going to talk to the owner about your situation. I can't make any promises, but let me see what I can do."

The following week he called me back.

"Pastor, we had our meeting. After representatives from multiple corporations made their proposals, I told our board the story of your church. I then looked around the room at everyone and said, 'You know, we sell to companies and other grocery stores all the time. Let's sell this building to the church if they can make the deal happen.' Everyone agreed. So, Pastor, the building is yours if you want it."

"When can we get inside the building?" I asked. He then made the necessary arrangements and set up a time for us to tour the facility.

GOD WILL CONFIRM HIS WILL IF YOU'LL ASK HIM.

The building was massive. The fact there were no walls and just one big open space made the 70,000-square-foot grocery store shell feel more like an old airplane hangar. Initially, I was very excited and filled with faith at all the possibilities. But those feelings quickly gave way to the same fear I had felt when I was in the mountains of Nicaragua.

What am I doing? I thought. *Are we really going to spend millions of dollars and move from our traditional-style church building to an old grocery store? What if no one comes with us?* Then I began to hear the voices of all the naysayers outside of our church and how they thought it was a bad deal to move to a grocery store. Even several other preachers had told me, "You ought to just stay right where you are. Why risk changing things when you're doing good where you are?"

Before taking another step, I grabbed Kaci's hand and began to pray. "Father, we desperately need to hear Your voice and know whether or not this building is Your will for us. Please show us what You're doing."

As soon as I had finished praying, we climbed the stairs and continued our tour through what was once the office area. Keep in mind, we were not in a church, a temple, or any other type of religious building. We were walking through the remnants of an old grocery store. Suddenly, as I turned the corner and walked into one of the offices, there hanging on the wall was an old, dusty plaque that looked like it had been there for years. The words written on it said:

"The will of God will never take you where the grace of God cannot protect you."

In that moment I knew the building was God's will. His timing was—and always is—perfect. Somebody going about their day-to-day routine had placed that plaque on the wall in a set time years earlier. God knew the exact moment and day that I—a preacher in need of direction—would walk into that old grocery store and need a word from Him. And that word was there waiting for me at the appointed time!

SEIZING THE MOMENT PRODUCES A BIGGER AND BRIGHTER FUTURE THAN YOU CAN IMAGINE!

Within a matter of months, we bought and renovated that old grocery store. The following year, over a thousand new people came and joined citylife church, and it became one of the fastest growing churches in America. Since relocating, over 4,500 people have become members. We don't just have one service—we have four! And we now also have multiple campuses. God is certainly doing an amazing work!

Did we honor our pledge to the pastor in Nicaragua and help build that church? Absolutely, as well as building many other churches around the world!

Looking back on our mission trip to that remote region, I believe we seized a God-moment in those mountains that launched us into multiple seasons of growth and effective ministry that we could have never dreamed possible. I believe God was saying, *If you're willing to invest and build a church for this pastor, you will thrust yourself into a new season of favor.* Our actions in Nicaragua built a doorway in Tampa, Florida, and God miraculously began a work that continues to expand and transform lives to this day!

What about you? What is God doing in *your* life?

Through the Apostle Paul, He says:

> Be careful how you act; these are difficult days. Don't be fools; be wise: make the most of every opportunity you have for doing good. Don't act thoughtlessly, but try to find out and do whatever the Lords wants you to (Ephesians 5:15-17 TLB).

I encourage you to stay alert! Don't just look and long for the next season. Keep your spiritual eyes open and seize the moments God places in front of you. There is power in the now! The unexpected connection, the random encounter, the door that opens suddenly could be the divine game-changer you've been waiting for to not only catapult you into your next season, but also unlock the door to seasons to come.

DISCOVERING YOUR DOORWAY

In light of the true story you just read about *seizing the moment*, reflect on and respond to these personalized thoughts and questions.

• What is my **greatest takeaway** from this chapter? What is most important to me in this moment that I want to remember?

____

____

____

____

• I believe the **action steps** God is prompting me to take are:

____

____

____

____

• Take time to **pray**: "Lord, is there a divine moment in front of me right now? If so, what is it? What fears are trying to keep me from stepping out in faith?"

Listen and *write* what He shows you. Ask Him to help you trust Him and praise Him, regardless of what you see or how you feel.

____

____

____

____

NOTES

"I know you well;
you aren't strong, but
you have tried to obey
and have not denied
my Name. Therefore
I have opened a door
to you that no one
can shut."

—Jesus
Revelation 3:8 TLB

8

IT'S YOUR TIME

So far, we've seen how the woman from the town of Shunem was actively seeking God with all her heart. Her mounting anticipation to see Him move in her life motivated her every decision. The Bible tells us . . .

- she attracted God's presence by inviting the prophet Elisha to stop in and eat the mouth-watering meals she prepared.

- she perceived God's anointing was on Elisha and caught a prophetic glimpse of the possibilities ahead for her.

- she forged a partnership with her husband, combining their gifts and resources to build a permanent space for Elisha to live.

- she and her husband kept stretching their faith, their finances, and their vision of what could happen through the entire process.

- she used what was in her hands to make room for more of God's presence, seizing the divine moments that were placed in front of her.

There was one more ingredient needed to bring about her breakthrough—an irreplaceable element that only God himself could contribute: His *timing*. While His plan is powerful and contains the details of where we're going, His timing is just as important. It's so crucial to guard our hearts against impatience—which pushes us to get ahead of God—as well as laziness and fear that will cause us to lag behind. When we learn to live in sync with what the Holy Spirit is doing, our life moves at just the right pace.

EVERYTHING IS BEAUTIFUL IN GOD'S TIMING.

When God's will, God's plan, and God's timing all collide, anything is possible. In fact, that's when truly supernatural things begin to take place. The impossible becomes possible, and what used to be only a dream starts to take root and becomes fruit in reality.

Ecclesiastes 3:1 says, "There is a time for everything, and a season for every activity under the heavens" (NIV). Then after giving us a long list of various activities, verse 11 says, "He [God] has made everything beautiful in its time. He has also set eternity in the human heart; yet no one can fathom what God has done from beginning to end" (NIV).

What does it mean that God has "set eternity" in our hearts? It means there are future plans for our lives that He has already set in motion, and as we are consistently obedient in what He is asked us to do, at the right time—the appointed time—what He has planned for us will begin to unfold.

THERE ARE TWO TYPES OF TIMING IN GOD'S WORD.

A careful study of Scripture reveals that God operates in two types of timing: *chronos* time and *kairos* time. The word *chronos* describes a "set time," and we find an example in the account of Creation (Genesis 1). For six consecutive days, the Lord created the heavens and the earth and everything in them. Everything came into being in a set, chronological order. With each passing day, the Bible says there was "evening and morning," showing a linear progression of events over time. *Chronos* timing is marked by days, weeks, months, and years—it's essentially time as we humans understand it.

The Bible goes on to say God has orchestrated "all nations of men to settle on the face of the earth, having definitely determined [their] allotted periods of time and the fixed boundaries of their habitation (their settlements, lands, and abodes), so that they should seek God, in the hope that they might feel after Him and find Him, although He is not far from each one of us" (Acts 17:26-27 AMPC). Here again is an example of God's involvement in our *chronos*—the set time He has choreographed for each of us to live in.

The second type of timing in Scripture is called *kairos*. This is when God suddenly and unexpectedly invades the *chronos* flow of our lives with a divine moment that's packed with supernatural potential to advance His kingdom and propel us into a new season. It's what I experienced in the mountains of Nicaragua when the Holy Spirit prompted me to help a pastor build a new church. Although that *kairos* moment was nowhere on my calendar, it was always on God's calendar, and He had been preparing me for it all along.

The same is true for you. If you've been faithfully living day by day, week by week, and month by month in God's *chronos* time, doing what He's asked you to do, rest assured that a *kairos* moment is coming your way. Although you can't see it right now, it is up ahead waiting for you. God is about to quickly move in and expand your life unexpectedly, and this appointed time cannot be stopped by anything the enemy tries to bring against you.

YOU CAN TRUST GOD'S TIMING.

When I think about God's *kairos* time, it reminds me of a situation that happened not too long ago. Out of the blue, I received an invitation from the White House, along with a group of influential pastors and religious leaders, to tour our nation's southern border. Immediately I felt it was a door of opportunity God had opened. In order to seize the moment, I immediately purchased a plane ticket and made plans to travel to McAllen, Texas—a town located on the Mexican border just west of Brownsville.

A few hours before I was supposed to fly out, I arrived at the Tampa airport on what looked to be a bright, sunshiny day. But as I was making my way through security and toward my gate, the weather began to change drastically. Dark storm clouds quickly rolled in, bringing powerful lightning strikes that delayed our flight and grounded our plane. Worry began to grip my mind as the winds increased, the lightning flashed, and the thunder crashed.

Am I ever going to get on this plane? I thought. *And even if I do, what if I miss my connecting flight in Texas?*

About an hour had passed, and it seemed extremely unlikely that I would make it in time to catch my connecting flight to McAllen. Knowing there were no other flights from Houston to McAllen that night, I went to the closest airline desk to explain my situation to the gate agent and let them know I was going to get off my flight. Much to my amazement, the lady knew who I was.

"Pastor Tony?" she said. "You don't know me, but my name is Jackie, and I've been attending citylife church for about six months. I so enjoyed your series on faith you just finished teaching! It was so powerful and life-changing for me."

I must admit I didn't recognize her, but I didn't want to make it obvious. So I smiled politely and listened to what she had to say. After a few minutes, she asked me what I needed, and I told her about the invitation from the White House and my trip to Texas.

"With all this severe weather and the delays," I said wearily, "I think I'm going to miss my connecting flight. So I think I'm just not going to get on this plane."

"Oh, Pastor Tony," she confidently replied, "I believe you're supposed to be on this trip. I'm going to pray and believe that you're going to make your connection without any problems."

Wanting to look like "super pastor," a man of faith and power, I said, "Okay, Jackie. Thank you." Then I went and sat back down.

A short time later, they finally let us board the plane. Once inside, however, we sat on the tarmac for another 30 minutes, with no sign of a liftoff in sight. Anxiously, I continued to monitor my airline app to track the status of my connecting flight and see if there were any other options available. When I could no longer contain my restlessness, I reached up and pushed the flight attendant call button.

"Yes sir," the attendant said. "What can I do for you?"

"I'm really concerned that I'm going to miss my connecting flight," I told him. "So I think the best thing for me to do is maybe get off this plane."

"Okay," he responded. "It doesn't matter to me. If that's what you want to do, get your bags."

Still wrestling with the decision, I called my wife, Kaci, and explained that I was about to get off the plane. She said, "Tony, I really think you're supposed to be on this trip. I'm going to pray that everything goes smoothly and you make your connecting flight in Houston."

"Okay," I answered reluctantly, and then hung up the phone and sat in the parked plane for another ten minutes.

At that point, the flight attendant returned and said, "Mr. Stewart, you're going to make your connecting flight."

"Are you sure?" I replied.

"I'm positive," he smiled confidently.

"Well, how can you be so sure?" I asked.

He looked at me and said, "The pilot of this plane is the pilot of your next plane. Your next flight can't take off until we arrive in Houston."

Sure enough, when we landed in Houston, we didn't even have to enter the airport. A car pulled up to the gate, and the pilot and I were picked up and driven to the next plane. He and I boarded the flight together before anyone else did.

When I look back on that season of my life, I was walking through some places that stretched and challenged my faith like never before. The Holy Spirit spoke to me through this situation and said, "Tony, I'm not only the pilot of *this season*, but I'm also the pilot of your *next season*. It can't take off until you arrive safely at the end of this one. The storms you're in will not stop your destiny or derail My plan for your life."

Without a doubt, my trip to the border was an incredible experience. I connected with some remarkable leaders who have become close friends. Within 48 hours, God opened some amazing doors, including an opportunity to go to New York City and be a guest on *Fox News Morning Show* and *Fox and Friends*. Not only that, but I also received offers from several other major news platforms in the weeks that followed. It was truly a journey full of God-moments.

My point is that no matter what you're going through right now, it's possible for you to be calm and not shaken. God is piloting this season of your life, as well as the next season, and every season after that. It's your time! God has you smack-dab in the palm of His hand, and no one can remove you from His powerful protection (see John 10:28-29). As dark as your situation may seem, know your *kairos* moment is approaching and will be here as surely as the promised blessing showed up for the woman from Shunem.

THE SHUNAMMITE EXPERIENCED A *KAIROS* MOMENT.

In the midst of a famine, the Shunammite woman recognized the presence of God moving in and through the prophet Elisha. When she perceived the Lord was about to do something and didn't want to miss out on it, she looked at her husband and said, "Let's work together and build a place for this man of God. I know our finances and circumstances might not look the best, but I sense this is a God-moment—an opportunity to invest in His kingdom that may not come our way again."

With this in mind, the Shunammite woman and her husband took what was in their hands and used it to build and furnish a room with everything Elisha would need. They not only attracted God's presence, but also created space for Him to take up residence. As a result, the longer Elisha stayed the more God's anointing permeated their house. Driven with a desire to bless the woman and her husband, Elisha turned to his servant one day and said, "Call her." When Gehazi had called her, she stood in the doorway. Then Elisha said, "About this time next year you shall embrace a son" (2 Kings 4:15-16).

Essentially Elisha said, "Your perception, your partnership, and your sacrificial stretching have not gone unnoticed. You've taken what you had in your hand and invested it in God's kingdom, and it's about to pay off. This time next year, a *kairos* moment is going to hit this house! God is going to give you something your heart has longed for, but your mind thought was impossible to receive. At the appointed time, God is going to bless you with a son."

YOUR *KAIROS* MOMENT IS ON ITS WAY!

Friend, what you may not have realized is that in every season up to this point, you've been building a doorway. Your prayers, your praise, and your perseverance have not gone unnoticed. When your finances and circumstances were much less than desirable, you kept investing, giving, and worshiping. In spite of overwhelming challenges, you've continued to obey God and resist the enemy. Your efforts are evidence of your faith, which has built a doorway to the *kairos* moment that is about to forever change your life for the better.

The naysayers and the devil cannot stop what God is about to do. It's your time. Disappointment is about to give way to delight. Sorrow and sadness will be swallowed by joy and gladness. God is saying, "Get ready! You're standing in a doorway, and it's your appointed time! The *kairos* moment that's been etched on My calendar since eternity past is about to invade your present. I'm about to slam the door forever on your yesterday and miraculously open the new door to your future."

So don't give up! Keep investing. Keep believing. Keep doing what you know God has asked you to do. As the Apostle Paul said so compellingly, "Let's not get tired of doing what is good. At just the right time we will reap a harvest of blessing if we don't give up" (Galatians 6:9 NLT). It's your time, so you can walk in confidence knowing that God is setting everything in place for the great opportunities, plans, and relationships He has ahead. The doorway to your destiny is about to open. Are you ready for the adventure?

DISCOVERING YOUR DOORWAY

In light of what you just read about God's timing, reflect on and respond to these thoughts and questions.

• What is my **greatest takeaway** from this chapter? What is most important to me in this moment that I want to remember?

___

___

___

___

• I believe the **action steps** God is prompting me to take are:

___

___

___

___

• Take time to **pray** something like: "Lord, please help me trust You when I find myself stuck in frustrating, stormy situations. Even though things look dark right now, give me the grace to keep my eyes fixed on You (see Hebrews 12:1). Thank You for proving that You're faithful by leading me and opening the new door(s) that You've had planned for me to walk through since the beginning. What can I be doing as I'm waiting to cooperate with You and be ready for what You want to do in my life? What do I need to remember on a regular basis to keep my faith built up?"

Listen and *write* what He shows you, knowing He has promised to direct and strengthen you no matter what, and you can trust Him (see Numbers 23:19; Isaiah 30:21; 40:31; 41:10).

____

____

____

____